W9-CHV-842

Riding

Riding

ROBERT OWEN
AND
JOHN BULLOCK

ARCO PUBLISHING, INC.
New York

Illustration acknowledgements
The photographs and artwork in this book
are the copyright of Newnes Books, with the
exception of the following:-
Animal Photography – Sally Anne
Thompson 12; Hamlyn Books 56 bottom.

Published 1985 by Arco Publishing, Inc.
215 Park Avenue South, New York, NY 10003

First published in 1984 by
Newnes Books, a Division of The Hamlyn Publishing Group Limited

© Copyright 1984 Robert Owen and John Bullock

All rights reserved. No part of this publication
may be reproduced, stored in a retrieval system
or transmitted in any form or by any means,
electronic, mechanical, photocopying, recording
or otherwise, without the permission of the
copyright owners and the publishers.

Library of Congress Cataloging in Publication Data

Owen, Robert, 1918-
  Riding.

  Includes index.
  1. Horsemanship.   I. Bullock, John.   II. Title.
SF309.094   1985   798.2   84-11038
ISBN 0-668-06284-3

Printed and bound by Poligrafici
Calderara s.p.a. Bologna

CONTENTS

INTRODUCTION

Horse riding as a form of exercise and recreation is continuing to develop in popularity, with people of all ages finding it an ideal way of enjoying leisure time. Horse ownership is also on the increase.

The sport – for that is what is has become with the immense competitive element – which was once considered a preserve of the privileged, is now within the scope of large numbers of people. This is evident from the considerable increase in the use being made of riding schools and other equestrian establishments, and the popularity of riding holidays which offer opportunities for riders at all levels.

As with every sport, a certain amount of basic knowledge needs to be acquired before the rider can achieve even a reasonable measure of enjoyment. Some who ride gain most of their fun away from the competitive scene and enjoy the freedom to be found by riding over open countryside. Even the highways can provide a welcome change from the confines and crowded atmosphere of city and urban life. Others like the excitement and challenge of competition, and for them there is a wide range of events, staged for all levels of ability, to satisfy even the most ambitious enthusiast.

Riding and the care of horses is such a wide and complex subject that any one book can only deal with certain aspects. This book has not been planned only as a beginner's guide; it is intended for those who already ride and those who have been away from the saddle and seek to refresh their memory of some aspects of horsemanship. All who ride are, however, strongly advised to continue to seek expert tuition. A book such as this can only outline the theory of riding; the question of proficiency and improvement will come by practical application, preferably from tuition given by those who have the necessary ability and teaching experience, and who have obtained the right qualifications.

In the pages that follow there are sections dealing with fundamental riding techniques which will, it is hoped, enable the less experienced rider to achieve balance, security, confidence and firmness in the saddle. The correct seat, and the use and application of the natural and artificial aids are dealt with at some length; most riders quickly become aware that most of the difficulties which arise between horse and rider come when the aids are not correctly applied, leaving the horse unsure about what he is being asked to do. Horse ownership is the natural development when riders set out to achieve a closer partnership and wish to become personally involved in every aspect of their horse's welfare and well being. However, circumstance must play an important part in horse ownership and people living in towns and cities are unlikely to have the essential facilities available. For these, keeping a horse at livery some distance away from home may be the only sensible answer. Even those who are fortunate enough to live in the country and have land and stabling available may be restricted by time and money, for keeping a horse fit demands daily attention. The time and facilities available must also have a considerable bearing on the type of animal to be bought, and the conditions under which it has to be kept.

The responsibility of owning and looking after a horse does, however, add a new dimension to riding, and every horse has to depend on his owner, or whoever is looking after him, for the right quality and amount of feed, water, care and exercise.

Everyone who rides would no doubt like to know how a horse is judged, and how to tell a good animal from a bad one. This is not easy – even for those who have spent a lifetime with horses. But it is important to learn the various terms and to appreciate what is meant by good or bad conformation, before being able to make any form of assessment. Other sections of *Riding* cover the important aspects of keeping and caring for horses and ponies both in stable and at grass, feeding, grooming, exercising, saddlery and equipment, and some of the different competitive disciplines that go to make up the world of equestrian sport.

Most horses are highly strung and somewhat nervous animals, yet they are intelligent and quick to react and respond. They are usually anxious to please provided that they are handled in a quiet, gentle and understanding way. It is this anxiety to please, and the confidence a horse develops in a rider, that tends to overcome his inbuilt nervousness and highly developed sense of self-preservation. Horses, like people, vary in size, temperament, strength and scope. They also vary in courage and ability. No two horses are exactly alike, and their likes and dislikes, their fears and weaknesses, have to be understood to get the best out of them.

Hacking in the countryside is enjoyable exercise for both horse and rider. Even for casual riding a hard hat should be worn, and it is a wise precaution to protect the horse's knees when riding on roads.

POINTS OF THE HORSE

In order to be able to describe the various parts of a horse quickly and accurately it is important to learn the correct terms, which are referred to as the points of the horse. Some, like the ears or the mane, will already be familiar, but it is important to know all the points in order, for example, to describe accurately an affected area to a veterinary surgeon, or to indicate the good or bad points of a particular animal to someone else.

1 Ear	13 Cheek	25 Stifle	37 Buttocks
2 Forelock	14 Shoulder	26 Shin	38 Dock
3 Forehead	15 Pectoral muscle	27 Chestnut	39 Hip joint
4 Eye	16 Forearm	28 Coronet	40 Thigh
5 Cheekbone	17 Knee	29 Hoof (wall)	41 Quarter
6 Lower jaw	18 Cannon bone	30 Heel	42 Croup
7 Nostril	19 Fetlock joint	31 Hollow of heel	43 Point of loins
8 Muzzle	20 Tendons	32 Fetlock	44 Back
9 Upper lip	21 Ergot	33 Hock	45 Withers
10 Lower lip	22 Girth	34 Point of hock	46 Mane
11 Chin groove	23 Belly	35 Gaskin	47 Crest
12 Bars of the jaw	24 Sheath	36 Tail	48 Poll

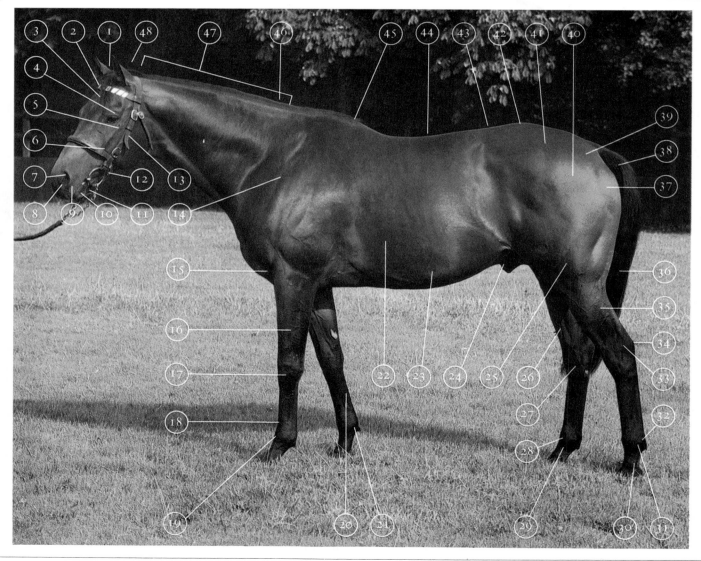

CONFORMATION

The conformation of a horse is all-important because it will show up any weaknesses and faults which may cause problems later. First impressions are important because the eye will take in the overall proportions of a horse and its general outlook. Having an 'eye for a horse' is the ability to notice its weaknesses and good points and to be able to judge its potential.

All parts of the body should form a harmonious whole and be properly in proportion. The head can tell a great deal about a horse's character. An eye that is bold with a kind, generous expression is generally a good indication of character. The eyes should also be placed wide apart. A fine, elegant head usually indicates a well-bred horse, while lop ears and a Roman nose frequently indicate a sensible and generous temperament.

The neck will give an indication of the horse's natural head carriage and should be properly in proportion. If it is too short it will make a rider feel insecure, and the horse will probably be more difficult to control. If it is too long it will be more difficult for the horse to support. The angle at which the head joins the neck is also important because it can affect respiration, and horses that are particularly deep from poll to jowl may find it difficult to flex properly without their breathing being restricted. An arched neck is the strongest and most elegant, but whereas a straight top to the neck can sometimes be improved by training, a ewe neck which has a concave line is usually a more permanent weakness.

The shoulder is also very important because it will give an indication of a horse's movement and pulling strength. A riding horse should have a long, sloping shoulder, which allows more freedom of movement and therefore a long, sweeping stride. A straight shoulder is more popular when looking for a carriage horse, because it provides more pulling power.

The back, being the weight-carrying area, will indicate the horse's strength and power. A short back will make the animal more stable and powerful, giving it a greater weight-carrying capability. A back that is too short, however, will not be supple, and may restrict its speed and action. Although a long back makes a horse supple, it needs to be muscular and broad to offset the weakness caused by its length, and the horse must have powerful loins. The shape is also important because although a back should be slightly concave, the hollow back sometimes found in older horses will be a sign of weakness. A sway-backed or a roach-backed horse will be unable to carry heavy loads.

The quarters provide the propulsive power a horse needs to be able to jump and gallop well. The upper line should be rounded and not flat, and the wider the quarters the more muscular power there will be. Quarters that are too wide, however, can result in a rolling action of the hind legs.

No horse's conformation is perfect, but the horse shown (*top*) is a good example of what to look for: compact body, strong legs, well formed neck and lively outlook. The elegant head (*above*) indicates a kindly disposition.

This lovely horse has considerable quality. Comparing horses of this kind – perhaps in the show ring – with other types will help the novice to acquire an eye for a good horse.

A relatively wide breast enables the forelegs to operate freely and also provides space in the chest for a good respiratory capacity. A deep, rounded chest has what is known as 'heart room' and the capacity for breathing deeply.

The forelegs have to take the strain of a horse's weight and also that of the rider, and must absorb the concussion that results from galloping and jumping. As a result they are the most common seat of lameness in a horse. The legs should be almost straight as far as the pastern, which should then slope obliquely towards the foot. The knees should not be shaped inwards or bowed, and should be clean, flat and well defined, though a horse that is 'over at the knee' puts much less strain on the tendons than one that is 'back at the knee'. The feet should also be straight, not turned inwards or outwards.

A horse should also have plenty of bone, which is measured at the circumfer-ence of the leg below the knee. The larger the circumference the better the weight-carrying capacity of the horse, and the flatter and more dense the bone, the greater will be the chances of the horse staying sound.

The fetlock joints should be broad enough to provide a good area of articulation, and round joints should be treated with suspicion. Any puffiness in the area of the fetlock joint is a warning sign of weakness. Pasterns should not be short and upright or they will produce a bumpy ride, while those that are too long and sloping will be weak and place too great a strain on the tendons.

Tendons are very important because they will be liable to give trouble to horses in demanding work. If there is heat and a hard swelling the tendon will probably cause continuous trouble, though heat and a soft swelling may be cured by rest.

Because the foot must be able to absorb jarring it should be round and open in shape, and not narrow, flat or too upright. It should be neither too big nor too small, and be free from cracks, rings and signs of brittleness and crumbling. The feet should also match each other in shape so

This horse is of a more cobby type; his calm and reliable approach would make him an easy ride and an ideal mount for a nervous or inexperienced rider.

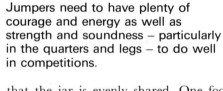

Jumpers need to have plenty of courage and energy as well as strength and soundness – particularly in the quarters and legs – to do well in competitions.

that the jar is evenly shared. One foot much smaller than the other could be a sign of navicular disease. The frog, the triangular wedge on the under side of the foot, should also be healthy and well formed because it is an important shock absorber.

A good hind leg is important because it is a source of power and propulsion, most of which is derived from the second thigh and the hock. A good second thigh is broad, strong, muscular and relatively long, and the hock should be wide from front to back; the bones should be neatly formed and well defined.

A good sound horse should never have 'cow hocks', when the points of the hock are turned in; 'bowed hocks', which are the reverse of cow hocks; 'sickle hocks', when the angle of the hock is very acute and the hind legs are in the shape of a sickle; 'straight hocks', which are the opposite to sickle hocks, or 'curby hocks', where a bony formation below the point of the hock can be seen from the side.

Few horses have perfect conformation. The main point to consider is whether any of the defects will affect the ability of the horse to work properly and remain sound.

CLOTHES FOR RIDING

Formal riding clothes consist of a dark blue or black jacket, white hunting stock, breeches and boots. For ladies a velvet cap or bowler hat is considered suitable; the bowler would be worn by men.

There is nowadays a more casual approach to clothes for everyday riding than there used to be, with the introduction of jeans, anoraks, hard rubber riding boots and various other comfortable all-purpose clothes. It is nevertheless useful to know about the appropriate traditional forms of dress, as for many equestrian activities such as hunting and all forms of competitive riding it is essential to wear the correct clothes.

Safety is now regarded as so important that forms of headgear are changing to allow riders to dispense with some of the more traditional, but not very strong or practical, types in exchange for riding hats with chin straps and skull caps with dark colours.

For everyday riding and informal competitions the traditional dress consists of breeches and boots, with hacking jacket and tie. Anoraks and sweaters should not be worn in the show ring.

With the new emphasis on safety, more riders are turning to crash helmets, with adjustable chin strap, for all cross-country riding.

MOUNTING
AND DISMOUNTING

If the horse is tall a beginner should make use of a mounting block when learning to get into the saddle for the first time. The stirrup leathers should be adjusted to suit the rider's height; the usual method for gauging approximately the correct length is to place the stirrup iron under the armpit and measure the length of the leathers against the outstretched arm. With the leathers taut the knuckles should just touch the spring bar, which is the piece of metal on which the stirrup leathers hang from the saddle.

It is normal to mount from the near (left) side, though it is as well to practise from both sides. Having made sure that the stirrup irons are down and the leathers are approximately the correct length, stand with the left shoulder next to the horse's near shoulder and take the reins and stick in the left hand facing the tail. Place the left hand in front of the withers and use the right hand to put the left foot in the stirrup. Press the toe down so that it comes under the girth and doesn't kick the horse in the side, which would have the effect of making him walk forwards, and pivot the body round to face the horse. Place the right hand on the far side of the saddle onto the front arch and spring lightly upwards, straightening both knees. Then swing the right leg over, making sure that it doesn't strike the horse, with the right hand still on the front arch of the saddle. Allow the seat to sink gently into the lowest part of the saddle and place the right foot in the stirrup, at the same time taking the reins into both hands.

To dismount, remove both feet from the stirrups and place the reins and the stick in the left hand. Put the left hand on the horse's neck and lean forward. Place the right hand on the front arch of the saddle, and swing the right leg back cleanly over the back of the horse, allowing the body to slip gently to the ground. Be sure to land on your toes,

bending the knees and avoiding the horse's forelegs, and then take hold of the reins close up to the bit with your right hand.

To adjust the stirrup lengths when mounted allow the legs to hang down and adjust the leathers so that the bars of the irons are on or slightly above the ankle bone. Riders should get into the habit of changing the length of the stirrups without looking down and without removing the foot from the stirrup iron. The best way of doing so is to take the reins in one hand, and with the other hand take hold of the spare end of the leather. With the thumb on top of the buckle steer the tongue of the buckle with the first finger, and with the other fingers continue to hold the spare end of the leather. Disengage the tongue of the buckle and guide it into the required hole. The buckle should then be moved up close to the bar of the saddle by pulling down on the inside of the leather and replacing the end.

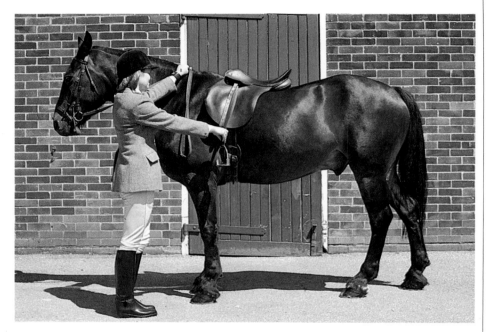

Preparing to mount: the rider stands by the horse's shoulder.

When mounted the rider should feel the weight of the body being carried equally on both seat bones, and be looking in the direction he intends to go. The body should be held upright and be supple without any tension. It is important that the hips, thighs and knees should be relaxed comfortably on the saddle so that the part of the leg below the knee can rest against the side of the horse.

The rider should always remain in balance with the movement of the horse, and this will entail supple hips, spine and shoulders. The ball of the foot should rest on the stirrup iron with the foot pointing forwards and the ankle slightly lower than the toe.

The hands must be able to move independently of the body, in harmony with the horse's mouth, and the wrists should remain supple without bending. A rider should have the same feel on the

With the reins gathered in her left hand and her left foot in the stirrup, she springs off the ground.

To dismount, both feet should be removed from the stirrups, and the rider leans forward.

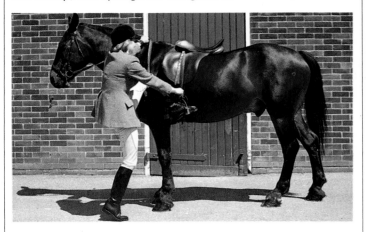

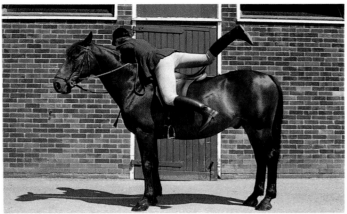

The rider should lean well forward so that her leg swings clear of the horse's back.

Again, the rider's right leg should swing well clear of the horse's back.

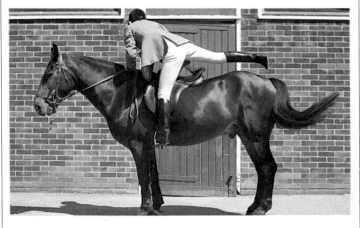

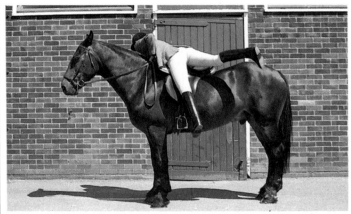

The rider settles gently into the saddle, taking the reins in both hands.

The rider has landed with her feet well clear of the horse's forelegs and in control of the reins.

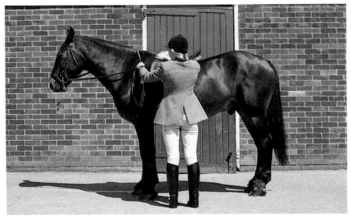

reins at all times; this feel is known as the 'contact', which must be neither too light nor too heavy, and must give a horse a secure feeling.

It is important that the hands should be carried with the thumb uppermost, and the backs of the hands pointing outwards. The wrists should never be allowed to stiffen or to become tense. The reins should pass directly from the bit between the little and third fingers, across the palm and over the index finger with the thumb on top. The third finger should hold the rein at the edges in the joints nearest the palm, with the fingers closed securely without tension. Holding the rein in the third finger stops it from slipping through the hands.

When holding double reins the little finger of each hand should divide the reins, with the bridoon (snaffle) rein usually held on the outside. To hold all the reins in one hand pass the reins from the right hand into the left so that the second finger divides them, with the slack ends passing over the index finger and secured by the thumb.

THE AIDS

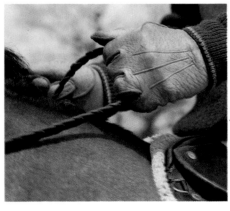

The natural aids: to communicate with the horse the rider uses the body, voice and changes in the distribution of weight, as well as the legs acting on and behind the girth and the hands in contact with the horse's mouth through the reins.

The 'aids' are the universal signals which rider and horse must both learn and understand so that the rider can convey his intentions to the horse. They must be given clearly and accurately so that the horse will be able to change pace and direction smoothly while remaining perfectly balanced.

In addition the term 'aids' also refers to the means at a rider's disposal for making the correct signals. There are the natural aids, which are given by the hands, legs, body and voice, and the artificial aids, which include sticks, spurs, and items of saddlery such as a martingale.

It is important for all riders to learn how to sit naturally and allow their body movements to blend harmoniously with those of the horse. The back muscles and the seat when used correctly can produce increased impulsion (power) and the rider must always remain in balance and be fully aware of the influence of the seat and body weight. The legs can also be used to increase pace and energy by pressing the thighs and the inside of the calves against the side of the horse. When riding in a circle the inside leg asks for impulsion with a quick, light, inward nudge, while the outside leg influences the horse's quarters.

The rider's shoulders and hands should remain supple to allow the hands to follow the movement of the horse's head, and to maintain an equal contact on the reins. The fingers of the inside hand will give directions with a quick take-and-give action, and those of the outside hand will control the speed and pace with the same action. The fingers of the outside hand also allow and control the bend.

The voice should be used to encourage, scold or soothe the horse, and may be used in conjunction with the other aids. For example, when the rider asks a horse to walk by creating impulsion with his legs, and controls the speed and direction with his hands, he can also instruct the horse to

'Walk on' with his voice, or he can praise his horse by giving a pat and saying 'Good boy' or 'Good girl' in an encouraging voice.

The most obvious of the artificial aids is the whip or stick, which may be used – with restraint – when a horse disobeys the rider's leg aids. The leg aid should be repeated and the whip used at the same time just behind the leg that gave the aid. For example, if the rider is asking for increased impulsion the stick should be used behind the rider's inside leg. It should be used behind the outside leg when the rider wants to control the quarters or strike off at a canter. The whip should always be used at the same time as the leg and should normally be carried in the inside hand. This is because it is the inside leg which is most frequently disobeyed. It will be necessary to change over the whip to the other hand when changing direction. To change the whip over in the simplest way pass it over the withers.

There are many types of spur. Those with rowels should never be used, but the blunt type have short or long necks and most have rounded ends. Riders using spurs must have a good independent seat and complete control of their legs; spurs are used by experienced riders to reinforce the leg aid and should only be used as and when required. They should be used without force by turning the toe slightly outwards and applying the inside of the spur against the horse's side.

Spurs are usually slightly curved and must always be worn point downwards with the longest side on the outside of the boot. The spur straps should be long enough to allow the spur to lie along the seam of the boot and should be the same colour as the boot. The buckle should be as close to the outside as possible.

The same horse and rider, but with artificial aids – a running martingale, stick and spurs – added. These should be used with discretion to reinforce the rider's commands.

EXERCISES FOR THE RIDER

There are various exercises which can be performed without stirrups that will help to strengthen muscles, improve the rider's balance and create a better seat. They should, however, only be practised for short periods, and should never be tried on an excitable animal. Some of the exercises can best be performed with a helper holding or leading the horse.

A simple exercise which can be done from the halt or the walk is to cross the stirrups over in front of the saddle, and leaning the body slightly forward from the waist, practise raising and lowering the seat. The position of the lower part of the leg should not change and the knees should not stiffen. Care should be taken to ensure that the reins are not used to pull yourself up from the saddle.

Without changing the position of the legs, place one hand on the rear of the saddle and the other on the horse's neck and turn to the left and the right,

When practising exercises in the saddle it is advisable to have someone holding the horse's head unless he is completely reliable. The rider should be prepared, even when performing exercises without stirrups, to re-establish contact with the horse at a moment's notice if anything goes wrong. It is also better to practise in an arena or other enclosed space rather than out in a large field.

changing the position of the hands to enable you to do so.

Turning the ankles both ways in a circular motion while they are still out of the stirrups helps to strengthen the ankles.

With the feet still out of the stirrups practise sitting down at the trot, but take care not to hold on by the reins or by gripping the saddle with the back of the calf.

Returning to the halt you should try bending the body slowly forward from the waist while looking up between the horse's ears, and then bend the body slowly backwards until the shoulders are resting on the horse's quarters.

Another excellent exercise for suppling the waist, which again should be done at the halt, is to hold the reins in the left hand and allow the right arm to hang down behind the thigh. The hand holding the reins should not be allowed to rest on the horse's neck, and you should then reach down and touch the right toe with the fingers. While doing this the seat must be well down in the saddle and the legs and arms remain in the normal position. Having touched the toe, you should come back into the upright position and repeat the exercise with the other hand. At first this exercise can be done with stirrups, but care must be taken to ensure that the position of the feet is not altered and that the legs are not drawn back.

The rider is performing various exercises to strengthen the seat and improve suppleness and balance; the text describes further exercises.

THE PACES

A horse that is moving correctly should look a picture of perfect harmony and grace. He should never look unnatural and should do everything with a minimum of effort, making him a pleasure to ride.

Horses are said to be in balance when their own weight and that of the rider is distributed in such as way as to allow them to use themselves with a maximum amount of ease and efficiency. Soon after they are born horses learn to balance themselves naturally, but when they are asked to carry a rider they have to learn to re-balance themselves. This is achieved by progressive training to develop the correct muscles.

When a horse has too much weight on his forehand he is considered to be out of balance, and the weight can be moved off his forehand by teaching him to supple his back and engage his hind legs properly.

Impulsion is the energy asked for by the rider, and supplied by the horse, and too much or too little impulsion may result in a horse losing balance. A horse is said to be going with the correct amount of impusion when he is willing to go forward in an active and vigorous manner with his back supple, his hocks engaged, without

When asking a horse to move forward into the walk a clear aid should be given and the horse encouraged to move off briskly.

24

tension, and mentally and physically relaxed. Impulsion should not be confused with speed, which is controlled mainly by a rider's outside hand, whereas impulsion is increased mainly by the rider's inside leg.

It is important for a horse to maintain the correct rhythm at all times, and to achieve this the horse must remain balanced. The tempo is the speed of the rhythm and the tempo of each pace must remain the same, and be maintained when the horse remains balanced.

From the halt the rider signals a horse to 'Walk on' by creating the right amount of impulsion with his legs, at the same time following the movement of the horse's head and neck with his hands.

As there are four beats to a stride the walk is termed 'four-time', and the horse always has at least two feet on the ground at the same time. When a horse walks he places his near hind, then the near fore, then the off hind, and then the off fore on the ground, in that order. The walk should always look and feel calm but at the same time be active and purposeful, and the hind foot should pass over the print left by the forefoot.

To go from the walk into the trot the rider should again create impulsion by a quick inward nudge with his legs, and at the same time let his hands go with the movement of the horse's head. There are two beats to a stride so the trot is termed 'two-time', and the horse moves from one diagonal pair of legs to the other with a moment of suspension between each step which should be regular and even.

Before moving from the trot to the canter the rider should ensure that his horse is trotting correctly and accepting the bit and going forward with the right amount of balance and impulsion. He should indicate with his inside hand the direction of the canter, sitting down for a few strides, and nudging the horse with the outside leg behind the girth.

There are three beats to the canter so it is termed 'three-time', and after the third beat there should be a moment of silence when all the horse's feet are off the ground at the same time. The canter should be light, balanced and rhythmic with considerable movement of the horse's head and neck.

When a horse is cantering to the right and leading with his off leg the sequence will be the near hind, then the off hind

and the near fore together, followed by the off fore. When cantering to the left and leading with the near leg the sequence will be the off hind, then then near hind and off fore together, followed by the near fore.

A horse should always canter 'true' or 'united', when the leading foreleg and leading hind leg will appear to be on the same side. He is said to be cantering 'disunited' when the leading hind leg appears to be on the opposite side to the leading foreleg.

The walk is a four-beat stride and should be energetic and purposeful. In the ordinary walk the rider should maintain even contact with the horse's mouth, encouraging him to adopt a correct head position and flex his neck at the poll in acceptance of the bit. After a schooling period a few minutes' walk on a loose rein, when the horse should be encouraged to lower and stretch his neck, will rest and relax him.

Schooling sessions may take place in an enclosed arena or out in a quiet corner of a field.

A request for increased impulsion while yielding a little with the hands will tell the horse to make the transition from walk to trot. The trot should be even and rhythmical, with a strong thrust from the horse's hind legs. Teaching a horse to perform the collected and extended trot will help to make him more responsive.

When increasing or decreasing the pace the rider should sit quietly in the saddle with the body absorbing the movement of the horse and absorbing any alteration in the pace, and making the correct contact with the legs and the reins. The legs should maintain the correct amount of impulsion and when asking a horse to slow down the pace the rider should make a quick take-and-give movement with the outside hand. Throughout the transition the horse must continue to accept the bit and should also learn to maintain the correct outline and balance.

When turning or circling the inside hand will again indicate the direction

During the canter the horse will need some freedom of his head and neck, though contact through the reins should be maintained. When cantering on a circle the horse should 'lead' with the inside leg for balance and comfort; when changing direction a few steps at the trot will enable the horse to change his lead.

required with a quick take-and-give movement, and the pace will be controlled by the outside hand. The inside leg should maintain the usual contact with the side of the horse in the region of the girth, while the outside leg should be placed behind the girth. To achieve increased impulsion the horse should be given a quick nudge with the inside leg. Throughout the movement the rider should sit in the lowest part of the saddle with the hips parallel with the horse's hips, shoulders parallel with the horse's shoulders, and the head looking in the intended direction. The horse must remain in balance and not lose tempo or rhythm.

SIMPLE SCHOOLING

It is important to ensure that the horse fully understands the instructions he is given, and so the more simple and clear the instructions, and the more familiar he is with them, the easier the horse will find the lessons in his schooling routine.

For this reason schooling sessions are important, but lessons should only be for short periods, and as soon as a horse has carried out his instructions correctly he should be made a fuss of and given some titbit as a reward. Before blaming a horse for doing something wrong, it is important to consider if the correct aids were given, or if he was asked to do something beyond his physical or mental capabilities. Horses, like children, are particularly sensitive to injustice, but if a reprimand is necessary it should be done quickly while he is aware of what he has done wrong. Whatever happens, never lose your patience or your temper.

After he has done his lesson well he should be allowed to do something that he really enjoys, like going for a hack or jumping a few simple jumps. Rewards, like punishments, are particularly meaningful to a horse, and patience and kindness, as well as rewards, are great assets when schooling. Firmness is of course important, and a horse that continuously misbehaves should be given a reminder with a stick just behind the girth, not in front of the saddle. Remember, however, that the stick is never a substitute for good hands and the correct use of the leg.

To develop suppleness and obedience schooling sessions should begin with work on the flat, and this can be followed by work over poles and cavalletti.

First of all get the horse to walk over the poles, which should have been laid on the ground about 5 ft (1.5 m) apart.

With five or six poles placed in a straight line about 4 ft 6 in (1.3 metres) apart ask the horse to 'Walk on', and on reaching the end turn him and walk back

Schooling sessions should be interspersed with more relaxed forms of exercise such as hacking, when the lessons can be put into practice away from the schooling arena, and horse and rider can also just relax and enjoy themselves.

Opposite: A good, strong rising trot. The rider should rise only slightly out of the saddle, and return to it gently, in rhythm with the horse's stride.

The sitting trot is often preferred during schooling sessions. The rider maintains closer contact with the horse through the seat and legs, so more effective control can be achieved; practising without stirrups is an excellent exercise for developing a strong, independent seat.

Walking and then trotting over poles laid on the ground is a useful exercise to improve the rhythm of the horse's stride, and is a good preparation for jumping.

over them using first the left rein and then the right.

The spacing of the poles can then be increased slightly to perhaps 1.5 metres depending upon the stride of the horse. Allow him to repeat the exercise at the trot. The poles can then be raised on bricks or blocks of wood to a height of not more than 6 in (15 cm) so that he has a series of small jumps to perform. Increased impulsion will be necessary, and the entire movement from one end of the line to the other should be done smoothly without any unevenness.

This type of schooling will help to teach the horse obedience and to develop his sense of balance and rhythm. It will develop the horse's natural eye and teach him mental and physical coordination. It will also develop the correct muscles by making him lower his head and neck, round his back, and engage his hocks. This also prepares him for further lessons in jumping.

Cavalletti make versatile first jumps. The height of the pole bolted to the end pieces may be varied by turning them over.

Single cavalletti make useful practice jumps, but they must never be built up to form higher obstacles. If one or two cavalletti are placed at the end of a row of poles on the ground the horse will learn to approach his fences calmly and with good balance, rather than rushing at them.

FIRST STEPS IN JUMPING

The act of jumping may be divided into four stages – the approach, the take-off, the jump, and the landing. During each phase the rider must suit his style to the movements of the horse, and throughout the whole of the jump he must remain in complete harmony with the horse.

During the approach the horse will balance himself by placing his head and neck forwards and downwards. The rider should sit still and lean slightly forwards, maintaining contact with the horse's head through the reins, and with his legs pressed against the sides of the horse, urging him forwards.

A horse takes off in two stages. First he pushes his forehand upwards by driving off is front legs and bringing the hind legs up underneath his body. The hindquarters and hocks then propel the body upward and forward over the obstacle. During the approach and take-off the rider should sit slightly forward and remain perfectly balanced so that he does not interfere with the movement of the horse. During the actual jump the horse will stretch his head forward and down while he is in mid-air, using his head and neck to maintain balance. Bringing his weight forward makes it easier to lift the

hindquarters over the jump, and the horse will raise his head and neck as the hindquarters come down and the forehand lands. The rider should follow all the horse's movements during the jump.

As the horse lands, his neck will stretch out and then lower again in order to

A relaxed and confident approach to a spread fence. It is important to present a horse straight at a fence, and to maintain good impulsion on the approach. When teaching horses to jump, wings should be used to discourage them from running out.

The horse's movements during the various phases of the jump – approach, take-off, the actual jump and the landing – are clearly shown here. The rider should stay in balance with the horse and maintain contact through the reins while giving the horse freedom to stretch out his head and neck.

enable him to go forward. The rider should remain slightly forward and in balance with the horse.

In order to be able to clear a fence cleanly the horse must take off at the correct place, and when approaching a fence the horse judges the point at which he intends to take off by looking at the line at the base of the fence, which is known as the ground line. Fences which rest on the ground, such as a wall, have a distinct ground line which makes them relatively easy to jump, whereas a single rail above

the ground has no ground line and is more difficult.

As horses usually tend to take off too close to a fence the obstacle will be made easier if the ground line is placed slightly on the approach side of the fence. If, however, the fence is composed of a single rail placed on the take-off side of a wall or a hedge, the horse will judge his take-off distance from the wall or the hedge at the base and will be more inclined to get too close to the rail. A fence like that is said to have a false ground line.

LUNGEING

Provided that a horse is fit, some trainers like to lunge for a short period each day as a means of suppling the horse, developing his muscles, action and balance, and getting rid of any excess exuberance.

When lungeing it is important to use the proper tack and to ensure that it is correctly fitted. The lungeing rein should be made of tubular webbing, about 25 ft (8 m) in length, and with a swivel billet at the bit end and a hand loop at the other. It can also be made with a swivel snap hook attachment which is fastened to one of the rings on the nose plate of a breaking cavesson.

The long lungeing whip with a light thong is also an essential part of lungeing equipment, as it is used to keep the horse moving forwards and away from the trainer. It should, however, only be shown to the horse, not used to hit him.

To circle the horse to the left, gather the rein in loops in your left hand, starting with the loop at the end of the lunge rein, and hold the whip in your right hand. Holding the horse by the cavesson on the near side you should start walking the horse round you in a small circle encouraging him to 'walk on', at the same time showing him the whip. This should not be used in such a way as to frighten the horse but just to make him walk on.

Make the horse walk in front of you all the time with the radius of the circle increasing. Young horses should be allowed a large circle; experienced, supple

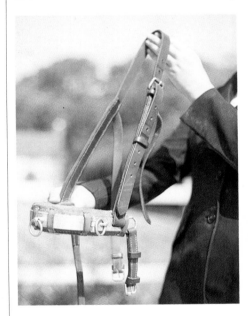

A lungeing cavesson (*above*) showing the swivel rings; the lunge rein is usually fitted to the centre ring. The horse and trainer (*right*) ready to begin work. Note the lunge rein correctly looped in the trainer's hand.

The lunge rein is gradually released as the horse begins to walk in a circle round the trainer. A young or unfit horse should be allowed a large circle; a fit and mature animal will be up to the greater demands imposed by a tighter circle. Side reins (*top right*) are sometimes fitted to encourage a correct head position on the lunge; they should be adjusted when changing direction so that the horse is able to flex his neck on the circle.

horses will be able to achieve a somewhat tighter curve. You should not walk after the horse or step backwards to keep the lunge rein tight, but keep turning round on the same spot. When the horse is going quietly, having at first walked and ultimately trotted or cantered, he should be slowed down and stopped by word of command, and brought into the centre towards you as you again gather the rein in loops in your left hand. Walk slowly back as the horse comes towards you, because horses of any age will come towards a person if they step backwards and not forwards.

After making a fuss of the horse, change the rein and whip into the other hand and repeat the performance going the opposite way. Lungeing sessions should last for no more than twenty minutes at a

time, and special attention should be paid to making the horse move round on the circle with long, regular strides and at an even rhythm. When a horse is asked to canter he must be encouraged by voice and whip to strike off evenly and calmly on the correct leg. If he starts on the wrong leg he must be checked at once, brought back to a trot, and started off again.

Care should be taken to ensure that the hind feet follow in the tracks of the forefeet. If there is too strong a pull on the lunge rein the horse's head will be turned inwards and the quarters and hind legs will move out off the line of the circle. At all times you must insist on obedience to the voice and the whip, and at the halt the horse must be made to stand square with his weight on all four feet.

CARE OF THE HORSE AT GRASS

The decision about whether to keep a horse or pony at grass or stabled may depend on the facilities available, and on the type and breed of horse being kept. Many ponies do better kept at grass, provided that they have adequate, well-fenced grazing which is not too lush in the summer, and there is plenty of fresh water and a suitable field shelter to provide protection from sun and flies in summer, and wind and driving rain in winter.

Sometimes the best solution for owners with only limited time available may be to stable their horse or pony for part of the time and turn him out when he is not needed. The secret is for the horse to be contented, and to be fit enough to be able to do everything that is expected of him without any strain.

A horse at grass cannot be turned loose in a paddock and left to fend entirely for himself, even though grazing is his natural way of life. Horses in the wild can forage and look for food over a wide area in the winter when grass is not available, but a domesticated horse or pony in an enclosed field has little opportunity of finding other food when the grass is short or the goodness has gone from it.

Grassland is affected by climate, height above sea level, soil and grass management. The grass a horse needs only grows well when there is sufficient moisture, warmth and sunlight, and its nutritive value will vary considerably from season to season. From autumn to late spring a horse will need extra food in the form of hay, and concentrates such as oats, bran and perhaps horse or pony nuts, whereas in the spring and early summer the grass will be highly nutritious and the danger will be that the horses may get too fat, and tend to eat too much lush grass. Very rich pastures are not good, and most horses and ponies will do best on more moderate land containing grasses such as meadow fescue, perennial rye grass, white clover, red clover and timothy grass.

Weeds such as thistles, stinging nettles and docks can be got rid of by regular cutting before they seed, or by spraying with weedkiller when the fields are being rested.

Poisonous trees and plants are usually a more serious problem than weeds, and a careful watch for them should always be

Many horses are more contented if they are kept at grass at least some of the time, as long as the pasture is properly maintained and they are still given adequate care and attention.

kept on fields where horses are being grazed; some plants, like ragwort, are deadlier dead than alive, and can be damaging to the liver of a horse. Plants that prefer damp ditches and hedgerows are more difficult to deal with, and are most dangerous when they begin to wilt, which is the time that most horses seem to prefer them.

Pastures can become horse-sick if they are not properly looked after, and tufts of long grass that horses won't eat are a tell-tale sign that something needs to be done. Pastures that have been over-grazed can also be a source of worms' eggs. Horses tend to deposit their droppings in certain areas, and if the droppings become infested with microscopic eggs from equine worms inhabiting an animal's gut they can quickly contaminate a field. The best solution is to graze cattle in the field and ensure that the horses are wormed at least three times a year. A horse with worms cannot get full benefit from the food he eats and will quickly become poor and listless. (Stabled horses should also be wormed regularly.)

If a field is not too large it is worth spending some time each week picking up the horse droppings in a wheelbarrow and taking them to a manure heap. Regular chain harrowing will help to disperse the droppings and at the same time expose the parasites to the cold and light. The field should also be rolled. If cattle or sheep are not available the areas of long grass should be topped either by hand or with a mower.

Each horse will required about 2 acres (0.8 ha) of pasture if he is to live out all the year round, and if you only have one large field it is as well to divide it in two so that

Common poisonous plants that can be dangerous for horses: (1) kidney vetch, (2) ragwort, (3) hemlock, (4) privet, (5) foxglove, (6) horsetail, (7) rhododendron, (8) ground ivy, (9) conifer, (10) oak acorns, (11) yew, (12) green bracken.

A well fenced pasture. Strong, thick hedges offer some protection from the wind as well as keeping horses securely fenced in. A wide, properly hung gate is easy to use.

one half can be rested while the other half is being grazed. The area of grassland required will depend on the type of soil: clay, for example, gets very wet and boggy during the winter, and horses are more likely to get mud fever, while in summer the clay becomes very hard and cracks appear. More grazing will be required with clay soil however much hay and concentrates are fed.

All grazing must be properly fenced, not only for the safety of the horses but also to prevent other people's property from becoming damaged by straying animals. Good sound hedges, free of poisonous trees and plants, or good post and rail fencing about 4 ft (1.5 m) in height with good gates and plenty of shelter are the most effective. Barbed wire, or wire fences that are not drawn tight, can be very dangerous; if wire fences are used the posts must be firmly fixed in the ground and the bottom strand should be not less than 18 in (50 cm) high.

A good supply of clean water is also essential. Domestic baths do not make good water troughs because horses can damage their legs on the lips, so if baths are used the sides should be boarded in. Field shelters need to be solid and have good wide openings and plenty of headroom. It is also important to ensure that they do not have any sharp protrusions. Horses enjoy a good rub from

Plain wire fences can be used, but they must be kept taut and safe (*above left*). Neglected fencing (*right top and centre*) is dangerous – escaping animals may be badly injured. The water trough (*left*) has been well sited to serve two paddocks; wherever possible troughs should be sited on firm ground to avoid the ground becoming poached (*above*).

time to time and a sharp nail or piece of metal can do a lot of damage. Corrugated iron roofs are not to be recommended because they get hot in summer when the horses want to get away from the flies, and are very noisy in the rain.

If horses start gnawing the bark off trees it is a sign that something is lacking in their diet, and it is always a good idea to keep a large lump of rock salt in the field. Good quality meadow or seed hay should be fed, preferably in a hay rack to keep it clean, but if the hay is fed in a hay net there must be one for every horse or pony in the field, and the net must be tied very firmly to a strong fence or a tree, and high enough so that a horse cannot get his foot caught in the net when it is empty and sags. The ground will get poached in wet weather wherever animals are fed, so it may be necessary to feed in different parts of the field. If hay has to be fed on the ground, which is wasteful because horses

A field shelter should be constructed to open away from the direction of the prevailing wind to offer maximum protection. Horses fed in the shelter are more likely to use it.

Catching a horse up from grass. Many horses will learn to come when they are called, particularly if some food is offered. The rope should be slipped round the horse's neck before the headcollar is fitted.

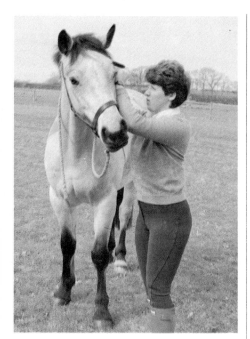

eat the best and spoil the rest, it should be placed in heaps in a circle if there are a number of horses to be fed or they will be inclined to squabble.

During the autumn and winter months horses at grass should be fed early in the morning and again about an hour before dusk, and a short feed should be given in the afternoon. It is important to try and feed at the same time each day because animals respond to regular hours, and if two or more animals are turned out together they will be inclined to begin milling around and get into trouble if they miss a feed or are kept waiting.

Concentrates should be fed in feed boxes, made preferably of wood or galvanized iron. There are portable galvanized mangers available which have two big hooks to hang over a stout rail in a fence, and these are excellent for feeding out of doors.

During frost and snowy weather the ice will have to be broken on the water supply at least three times a day because a horse is unable to break even thin ice by himself. When the ground is frozen unshod hooves are more inclined to crack and break, so the services of a blacksmith may also be needed.

Horses and ponies can be difficult to catch when turned out, and it is as well to get them into the habit of coming to call and rewarding them with a titbit such as a piece of apple or carrot or a bit of bread. If it is necessary, as a temporary measure, to leave a headcollar on a horse it must be fitted correctly, with three fingers' width being allowed round the noseband so there is room for the jaws to move freely when the horse eats. Always use a browband to prevent the headcollar from slipping back and rubbing the mane, and

ensure that the headcollar is soft and well oiled.

When turning a horse out, try to prevent it from galloping away immediately it gets in the field. Take enough time to shut the gate and lead the horse about ten yards into the field. Turn him round to face the gate and make him stand while you pat him and perhaps give him a titbit before taking off his halter. Then walk right away. If more than one pony or horse has to be let into the field at the same time make sure that they are all released together and kept well apart.

If a horse has been working and has returned home hot, or if it is wet, it should be turned out as quickly as possible and not left in a stable where it can get cold. Take off the saddle and bridle, put on the

headcollar and give the horse a chance to stale. Rub the saddle patch and behind the ears with a handful of straw or hay to help restore the circulation, and offer him some cool but not very cold water. Don't worry if he doesn't drink the water, just make sure he doesn't have any knocks, cuts or thorns, and then turn him out. He will probably get straight down and roll, have a good shake, nibble a few mouthfuls of grass, go for a trot, and then have a drink. That is nature's way of easing tired muscles and getting warm and dry if he had been sweating and might now be getting chilled. He should always be caught again the following day and checked over for cuts and any other injuries, and to have the remaining sweat marks brushed off.

THE STABLED HORSE

Horses or ponies kept at grass will need daily attention, but their requirements will be modest compared with those that are stabled. A stabled horse will need daily exercise and grooming and at least three feeds a day, and the stable will have to be mucked out regularly. He will also need rugs to keep him warm, and probably more frequent visits from the blacksmith.

Stables need not necessarily be expensive, but they should be of the right size, and be draughtproof, light, airy and well drained. They should also have no low beams or projections on which a horse could injure himself, and be strong enough to withstand half a ton or more of horse leaning against the sides and the doors, or kicking against the sides when he gets down to roll. The stable fittings must also be safe and adequate.

Stalls are less popular than they used to be and most horses are now kept in loose boxes, where they have freedom of movement. Loose boxes should have about 10 ft (3 m) of headroom, with a floor area about 12 ft (3.5 m) square. This amount of space allows a horse plenty of room to lie down, is economical as far as bedding is concerned, and is also easy to keep clean. A horse might bang his head if the height is reduced, and because there would be less air the stable could get too hot in summer. Horses sometimes seem to get themselves into more trouble in very large stables. They are more inclined to be careless when they roll and get themselves 'cast' – stuck against the wall so that they cannot get up without assistance.

Brick-built stables and those built of solid concrete blocks are of course the best. They usually look nicer, last longer, and because they have better insulation they are usually warmer in winter and cooler in summer. They are also more inclined to be rat proof. Because of high building costs, however, wooden stables have become very popular. They must be very well constructed, and have a wide enough canopy running along the front to provide shelter against the rain and the sun. Most wooden prefabricated stables have been treated against rot, but they need to be lined with strong boards to a height of about 5 ft (1.5 m) to prevent the walls being damaged. Roofs are usually made of wood covered with felt or tiles; corrugated iron is not to be recommended because it gets too hot in summer and is also very noisy in wet weather.

The importance of adequate ventilation cannot be over-emphasized: horses need plenty of fresh air to remain healthy.

THE STABLED HORSE

Opposite: A well planned wooden stable block. The overhanging roof provides shelter from the rain and shade from the sun both for the horses and for their attendants.

Left: One of these stable doors has been fitted with metal sheeting to prevent damage by the horse. Note the kick-catch at the bottom of the doors.

Below left: Hay fed in nets is easily carried over the shoulder. To the right of the photograph some stable equipment can be seen, including fork, rake and skip trolley.

Below right: Tying a hay net in the corner of a light, well ventilated loose box. The bedding is banked well up round the sides of the box.

Doorways should be some 7 ft 6 in (2.3 m) in height, and be wide enough for a fully tacked-up horse to pass through without damaging the saddle or hurting himself. They should open outwards in two parts so that the top can be left open, with the bottom half about 3 ft 3 in (1 m) in height with metal sheeting at the top to prevent the horse from chewing it. They need to be fitted with proper stable bolts with a kick-catch at the bottom. All light switches and fittings must be of the safety variety and out of reach of the horses. Windows need to be barred or covered with wire mesh, and should be hinged at the bottom to open inwards.

Apart from tie rings few stable fittings are necessary. Mangers are difficult to keep clean and bits of stale food, apart from being bad for the horse, also encourage rodents. Feed bowls, which can be placed on the ground, are far better, and the floor is the horse's more natural feeding position. When the horse has finished the bowl can be removed and washed ready for the next feed. A hay net prevents hay from being wasted, but the tie ring needs to be high enough to prevent the net from getting near the horse's feet when empty and not so high that hay seeds can fall into his eyes. Automatic water bowls save time, but

good strong plastic buckets within sight of the door enable one to tell exactly how much water a horse is drinking, and they can be removed before a horse is due to do fast work. Water buckets need to be checked at least three times a day and should each have a capacity of at least 2 gallons (9 litres).

Unless straw is dust free and of good quality other types of bedding are often more satisfactory, and are easier and quicker to deal with. Straw looks and smells nice but it also has the drawback of being pleasant to eat which means that some horses are prone to eating their bedding, and there is little point in trying

Right: The muck heap should ideally be situated in an unobtrusive corner some way away from the stables. If it is constructed methodically it will not become a sprawling pile.

Below: Shavings make a popular alternative to straw for bedding. Droppings and wet bedding can be removed either with a fork or by hand using stout rubber gloves.

Bottom: If the stables do not have water individually piped to them it will have to be carried; the weight is easier to manage if two buckets are carried.

to ensure that a horse has a balanced diet if he eats his bedding. Most of the straw bales produced by modern methods contain a great deal of dust and chaff. Wheat straw is preferable to barley or oat straw as long as it is dry and free from mould, and is light gold in colour.

Many owners prefer shavings, which are easy to skip out, and although some horses will nibble at them before the new shavings have been mixed with the existing bedding they will not normally eat them. It is important, however, to ensure that the shavings are of good quality, free from dust and bits of wood. Before shavings are used for bedding the stable drains should be covered to prevent them from becoming blocked, and to ensure that a good depth of shavings can be maintained.

The equipment needed in a stable yard will depend on the type and variety of bedding being used. A good-sized wheelbarrow, a shovel, a four-pronged dung fork, a bristle broom and a skip are essential, though a large plastic bowl can take the place of a skip. A pair of strong rubber gloves and a metal rake can also be useful when shavings or sawdust are used.

The tack room should be warm and dry and as thief proof as possible. It will need to be fitted with enough saddle racks and bridle cups to cater for whatever saddlery is required. A vermin-proof box for storing unused rugs and blankets, and a cupboard for keeping boots, bandages and cleaning materials will also be needed.

The fodder store, with its vermin-proof containers, should also be near to a fresh water supply, and the hay barn needs to provide protection from the weather. For safety it should ideally be some distance away from the main stable block.

PRINCIPLES OF FEEDING

Grass is the natural food for horses, and grazing in a field is the natural way for them to eat. A stabled horse, however, has no opportunity to graze, except on the occasions when he is allowed a special treat, and it is consequently important to ensure that he has a balanced diet and is fed at regular intervals each day.

Horses have a very small stomach for their size, and unlike that of a dog it will not stretch very much. A big meal may give a horse colic, so little and often is the feeding policy to follow. A horse should never be kept without food for more than four or five hours at a time, because if he is forced to wait too long between meals he will be inclined to bolt his food and the stomach will become overloaded because it will not be able to deal with the meal in the way nature intended.

Some horses require more food than others even though they are doing the same amount of work, and this variation should be taken into account when planning a horse's diet. To judge how to feed a horse properly it is important to understand the animal's natural way of life, how his digestion works, and how his food is used. How much to feed and the type of food to give is frequently a matter of trial and error. Like people, horses can be fussy eaters, and what suits one horse may not suit another.

The amount and type of food that should be fed will depend on the kind of work a horse is expected to do – as well, of course, on his size. In the case of a new horse it may be possible to discover from the previous owner whether the horse has any particular likes and dislikes and how much he was being fed.

Horses doing strenuous work such as hunting, show jumping, eventing or racing can have a higher proportion of concentrates like oats, bruised barley or horse nuts; oats should never be fed to small ponies or to horses in light work. The daily ration of concentrates should be

split into two, three or even four meals a day. Because horses are creatures of habit they need to be fed as far as possible at the same time each day, though this may not always be possible with competition horses.

Morning, noon and evening are the best times to feed a stabled horse, and this

It is vital that the feed room should be kept immaculately clean, and free from vermin. To ensure that each horse is fed exactly what he needs, it is wise to weigh out the feed.

Hay should be stored off the ground; simple wooden planking will be sufficient. If it is fed in hay nets it is a simple matter to check the weight appropriate to each horse.

should fit in with his periods of work. A further feed may be given at night. Stale or poor quality food will do more harm than good, and must never be fed. Mouldy or dusty hay can cause respiratory problems as well as colic and will always prove to be far more expensive in the long run than costly but good quality hay.

Some owners like their horses to have all the hay then can eat. Others prefer to give a small amount of hay with the early morning meal, at least two hours before

the horse is due to be exercised. Hay can be fed again after the morning's work, and the remainder of the ration can be given at night after the final feed of the day.

Horses like to be left alone when they are eating, and the manner in which the food is given to them is always important. A pat and a kind word will do more to ensure that a horse remains a 'good doer' than throwing the food in to him.

Hay should be fed in hay nets if the horse is bedded down on straw unless the stable has a satisfactory hay rack. This

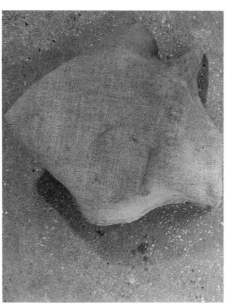

Above: Making a bran mash. A full measure of bran and a handful of salt are put in a bucket and saturated with boiling water. The mixture is stirred and left to soak and cool under a piece of sacking or thick cloth. It will be ready to feed when it is comfortably warm to the wrist or elbow – and should be well stirred before being tested to ensure that it is the right temperature throughout. A mash can be made more tempting by sprinkling a few oats on the top.

Left: Horses' teeth periodically need attention; a veterinary surgeon will rasp them if they become unduly sharp or unevenly worn, or if the horse shows signs of discomfort while it is eating.

will prevent the hay from becoming trampled in with the straw, which will not only be wasteful but also encourage a horse to eat his bedding. Hay is best cut in the early summer before it loses quality. There should be plenty of leaf and flower to show that it was cut before the grass had gone to seed, when much of its nutritional value is lost.

Oats are the best food for promoting energy and developing muscle. There are many varieties of colour, including black, white and grey, but the colour will not matter provided that the grains are short and plump and there are not too many husks. They should always be fed bruised or crushed, never whole, though some people prefer to buy whole oats and have them crushed before they are delivered so that they can see their quality beforehand. Barley can be judged in a similar way to oats, and it should always be fed to horses after the barley has been bruised because it is indigestible to them if the

husks are not cracked. It should also be boiled and allowed to soak for some hours before being fed. Boiled barley is often mixed with bran and other concentrates and can be used to help the condition of a horse that has been off colour.

There are many other foods a horse will enjoy provided that they are fed correctly, including flaked maize, beans, sugar beet, molassine meal, linseed, apples, carrots and of course horse nuts or cubes. Variety in a diet is important because many horses do not like eating the same food every day. Chaff, which is usually a mixture of hay and good quality oat straw cut into short lengths, makes fine roughage. When mixed with a feed it will encourage a horse to chew his food more thoroughly.

Bran on its own also makes an excellent mash and is very useful for a sick or tired horse, or one which is not being worked for a day or two. It should always be fed after hunting, and a stabled horse should be given at least one bran mash a week.

THE IMPORTANCE OF GROOMING

Horses at grass should not be groomed too thoroughly in winter because they will need the natural grease in their coats to help protect them from the weather. A dandy brush or rubber curry comb to take away the mud, particularly in the areas covered by the saddle and bridle, and a hoof pick to clean out the feet, are probably all that will be required. During the summer, however, there is no reason why a horse at grass should not be given a good daily grooming.

A horse moults twice a year: in the spring when the sleek summer coat is grown, and in the autumn when the short hairs are replaced by the longer and more greasy winter coat. When a horse is out in a field and the weather is really cold, the hair will stand on end, increasing the layer of warm air trapped inside and so improving the insulation against the cold. That is why once the coat is dry the sweat marks where the hairs have become stuck together should be brushed out, or the hairs will not be able to stand up properly.

Grooming not only makes a horse look smart, it also improves the circulation, tones up the muscles, helps to prevent disease, and maintains the horse in good condition. It should follow a routine that ensures that every part of a horse is dealt with in turn. In winter grooming will probably have to be done in the stable, but when the weather is fine it is more pleasant to do it outside in the shade.

After tying the horse up on a short length of rope, start with the hoof pick and clean out each foot in turn. Begin at the heel and work the hoof pick towards the toe, taking care to clean the grooves on either side of the frog. Clear the cleft of the frog, and look for any signs of trouble like thrush, which is a disease of the frog that has a nasty-smelling discharge. Put the dirt and loose stones into a dung skip instead of letting the muck lie on the floor for him to tread in. Tap each shoe in turn to see that they are secure, and run a

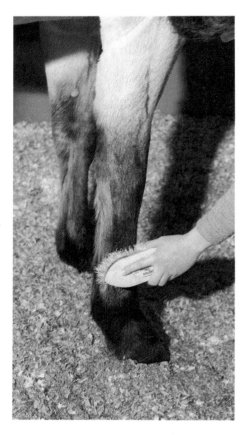

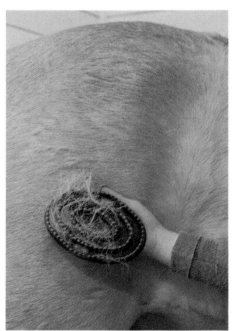

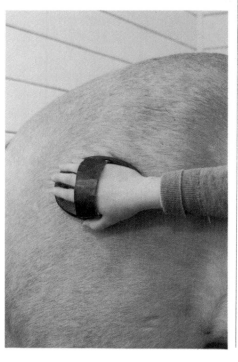

finger round the wall of the hoof to check that the clenches, which are the ends of the nails, have not risen.

Then take the stiff-bristled dandy brush, and beginning on the near side at the horse's poll, work the brush in a to-and-fro motion until you have gone all over the body removing all the caked dirt and sweat marks. Care should be taken when brushing in the region of the loins and other tender parts, and on bony areas such as the legs.

The body brush, which should be used next, has short, close-set hairs which are designed to reach through the coat to the skin. Except when it is being used on the mane and the tail, the body brush should be worked mostly in short circular strokes

50

It is important to learn how to tie a secure quick-release knot. The rope is tied not to the ring but to a short loop of string; if the horse struggles and pulls away in fright the string will break rather than the horse being injured or breaking its headcollar, or the ring being pulled away from the wall.

Opposite: Grooming a grass-kept horse. It is essential that the natural protective oils in the horse's coat are not all removed, so very thorough grooming is not required. The feet should be picked out and inspected (see page 52); the body and legs may be brushed free of mud; a rubber curry comb is useful to remove sweat marks and loose hairs.

in the direction of the lay of the coat. After every half a dozen strokes the brush should be drawn across the curry comb to remove the hairs and dust.

When the curry comb becomes full it may be emptied quite easily by means of a gentle tap on the floor. The headcollar will have to be dropped and the headstrap fastened round the neck in order for the head to be brushed. The brushing should be done gently using the free hand to steady the head.

The dandy brush should never be used on the tail or the mane because it will only break or remove the hairs, making the tail in particular appear thin and unsightly. The softer hairs of the body brush may be used, however, although some people like

to use their fingers, particularly on the tail.

The horse will then be ready for his body massage, and for this you will need a wisp made of woven hay or one of the leather pads with a strap across the back, which are sold by many good saddlers. The massage will develop and harden the muscles and give a shine to the coat by squeezing oil from the glands of the skin. Dampen the wisp slightly – the pad can be used dry – and bring it down firmly in the direction of the lay of the coat. Special attention should be given to the parts where the muscles are hard and flat, but it is important to avoid all the bony prominences and the tender regions of the loins.

Next dampen the sponge in the bucket of water and gently wipe the eyes, working away from the corners and around the eyelids. Wring out the sponge and wipe the muzzle area including the lips and inside and outside the nostrils. After again washing out the sponge lift the tail as high as possible with one hand and clean the whole of the dock region, including the under surface of the tail; horses appreciate the refreshing effect of the sponging as long as it is done carefully. Some people prefer to keep a separate sponge for the dock area.

The water brush should be dipped in water and used to flatten the mane, brushing the hairs from the roots downwards. The water brush can also be used to wash the feet, but if the wet brush is used the thumb of the hand holding the hoof should be pressed well down into the hollow of the heel to prevent any water from going in there. When the hooves have dried they can be brushed over with hoof oil with the help of a small, clean paint brush. The oil not only improves the appearance but also helps to prevent broken or brittle feet.

Finally, a stable rubber should be folded flat and used to go all over the horse to remove all traces of dust. The rubber can be dampened slightly to make it more effective.

The full grooming routine shown here should be carried out daily on a stabled horse. Most horses enjoy the process and are cooperative, though those with particularly sensitive skin may be ticklish.

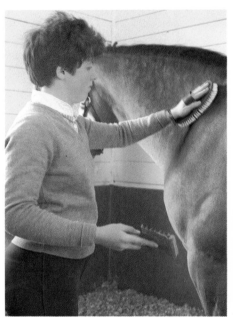

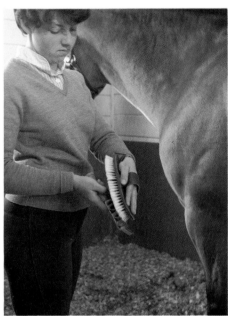

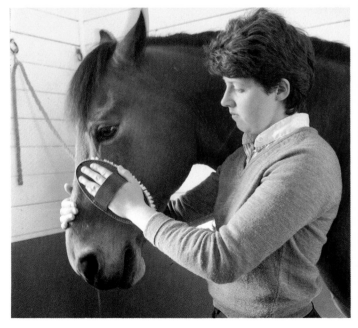

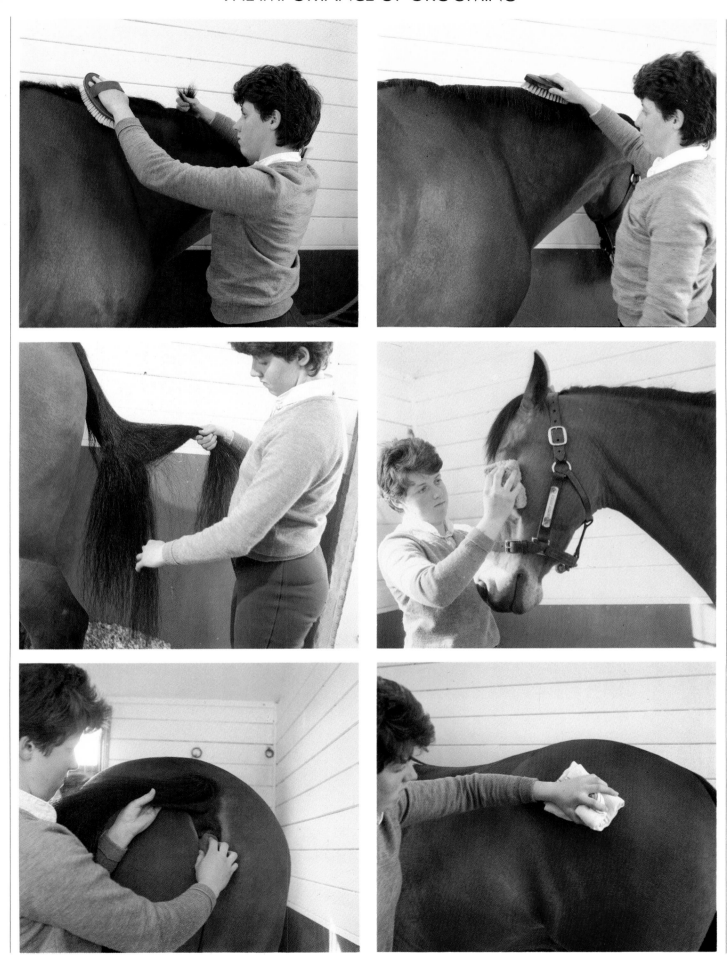

PLAITING, TRIMMING AND CLIPPING

Plaiting is done to improve the appearance and to show off the horse's neck and crest. It helps to make the neck look neat and trains the mane to fall onto the correct side, which is normally looked upon as being the off side. There should always be an uneven number of plaits down the neck, and one plait for the forelock. A hunter should have a minimum of six plaits altogether.

To plait correctly you will need a water brush and a little water, some lengths of thread about 8 in (20 cm) long, a mane comb, a pair of scissors, and a needle with a large eye.

First dampen the mane with a wet brush and divide it up into the number of plaits you intend to have along the mane. Then start on the first plait, and when you are about three parts of the way down take one of the pieces of thread and double it over before starting to plait it in. When the plait is complete the ends of the thread should be looped around the plait and pulled tight. By the time you have completed all the plaits they should all be the same length; if one is longer than the other make a further loop over. Then thread both ends of the thread through the eye of the needle, double the end of the plait under, push the needle through the

plait near the crest from underneath, and pull the ends of the thread through. Finally remove the needle, bind the thread tightly round the plait, and finish by knotting the thread on the underside of the plait and cutting off the spare ends of thread with the scissors.

If the mane needs to be thinned out before plaiting because it is too thick or long, it can be pulled by removing the longest hairs from underneath a few at a time. This can either be done with the fingers or by winding a few hairs round the comb and plucking them out briskly. Never pull the top hairs or any that may be left standing up after the mane has been plaited, and never cut the mane.

A well-pulled tail also adds greatly to the tidy appearance of a horse, but horses kept at grass should not have their tails pulled because doing so will deprive them of natural protection in the dock area.

First remove the tangles and separate out the hair. Then begin pulling at the dock region by removing all the hair from underneath. When that has been done work sideways removing the hair evenly on both sides of the tail, again by removing only a few hairs at a time. If you are planning a 'bang' tail get someone to put their arm beneath the root of the tail

so that the tail stands out in its natural position and then cut it off square about 4 to 8 in (10 to 20 cm) below the point of the hock. A switch tail will need further pulling, to about half the length of the tail, so that the ends of the tail can grow to a natural point. After being pulled the tail should be bandaged, but the bandage must never be put on damp as it shrinks on drying and could restrict circulation in the dock.

Plaiting a tail is a useful alternative to pulling if a horse is at grass or if he resents his tail being pulled. The hairs in the dock

Plaiting a horse's mane requires some practice for a really neat effect to be achieved. These photographs show precisely how to follow the various steps described in the text.

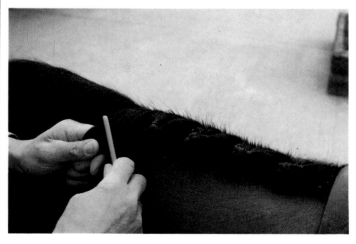

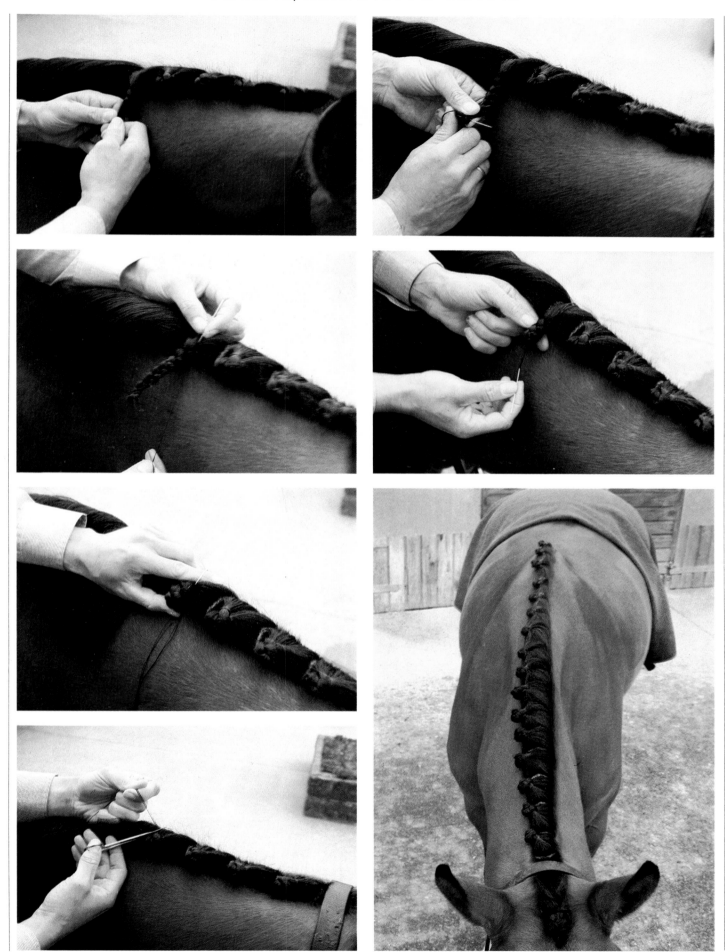

Clippers should be well oiled and sharp to deal effectively with a growing winter coat. There are various types of clip: *below left*: the trace clip, which leaves the horse some protection; *below right*: the blanket clip; *bottom left*: the hunter clip, *bottom right*: the full clip.

region must be allowed to grow long so that a small number can be separated with the finger and thumb on either side of the tail and knotted together with thread. The knot should hang down the centre of the tail, and successive small bunches of about ten hairs at a time from either side can then be plaited with it. The plaits should go down about two-thirds of the dock, and then only the centre hairs of the tail should be plaited, forming a pigtail. The end of the pigtail should be secured with thread and looped back underneath to the point where the side hairs are included; the loop should then be stitched together to form one plait.

A heavy winter coat can be a disadvantage to a horse that is expected to work because it will cause him to sweat too much and lose condition. To prevent this from happening the coat can be clipped, which will allow him to work longer, faster and better, and he will dry off more quickly. A clipped coat also saves time when grooming, helps to prevent disease, and makes it easier to detect a cut or a swelling.

The summer coat, being fine and short, should never be clipped. The winter coat is usually given its first clip in early autumn, and as it will grow quite quickly it will need further clips at least every three months or whenever the coat is more than a centimetre in length. The last winter clip should take place before the summer coat has started to come through.

Make sure that the blades are well oiled and that the clippers are sharp. The clippers should be used in the opposite direction to the way the hair grows, keeping as level a pressure as possible. The person doing the clipping should wear rubber-soled boots or shoes, and long hair should be protected with a headscarf.

Heels can be trimmed barber fashion by using a comb and curved scissors. The hair on the back of the heels should not be cut too short or the skin will become chapped and the horse may get cracked heels.

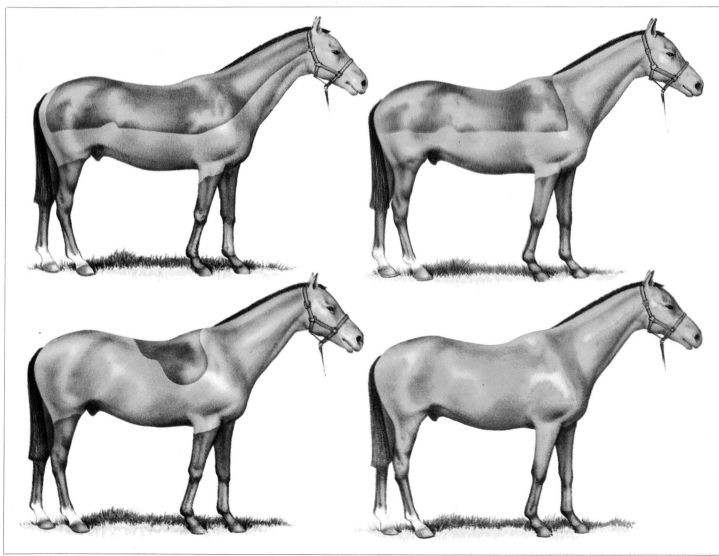

No Foot- No Horse

A good experienced farrier is an essential member of the team needed to keep a horse fit and well, and also to help cure any ills that affect the feet. A horse in work ideally needs to have his shoes removed about every three or four weeks, even if they are not worn enough to need to be replaced with a new set.

Shoes help to prevent soreness caused by the hard surfaces of the roads and stop the hoof from breaking, but because they are bound to have some effect on the natural functioning of the feet the way in which a horse is shod is of great importance. A number of bones are encased within the hoof, with areas of sensitive flesh around them known as laminae. Although the walls and the soles are rigid, the inner part of the foot is capable of limited movement because of the rubber-like quality of the frog. The frog takes much of the horse's weight, and absorbs the concussion when the foot comes in contact with the ground. As it does so it becomes compressed, expands, and forces the end of the wall slightly outwards, enabling the inner structure to move.

When a hoof is damaged its stiff box-like frame causes problems because it cannot swell in the way that other parts of the body can when subjected to severe concussion or abnormal strain. This inability to swell can give rise to serious complications which may, in some instances, aggravate the condition to such an extent that the bones become deformed or pushed out of place, and a horse made permanently unsound.

The wall of a healthy hoof grows at the rate of more than $\frac{1}{2}$ in (1 cm) a month, so the shoes have to be removed regularly to prevent the foot becoming misshapen, and to prevent additional strain being placed on the fetlocks, tendons and suspensory ligaments.

When the blacksmith removes the shoe he will first of all look to see whether any

part has had undue wear, which will tell him whether something should be done to correct a fault in the horse's action. He may have to build up or lower the sides of the shoe to get the horse's weight distributed more evenly. Before replacing the shoe or putting on a new one, he will cut down the wall of the hoof and rasp it level, being careful not to damage the frog or the sole of the foot. The shoe should always be made to fit the foot and not the foot to fit the shoe, whether the blacksmith is using the cold shoeing or the hot

A farrier at work with anvil and hammer, shaping a shoe. A skilled farrier is essential to keep horses' feet healthy and strong and to help with remedial shoeing when necessary. Shoes will have to be replaced every five or six weeks, and often more frequently than this on horses that live in towns and are worked mostly on roads.

shoeing method. Cold shoeing is when the shoes are made up beforehand, and not heated in the forge and altered before being nailed to the hoof. It is never as satisfactory as the hot shoeing method but if the blacksmith knows the horse well and makes up the shoes specially beforehand there are unlikely to be problems.

With hot shoeing each shoe is heated until it is red hot, and by holding it onto the hoof the blacksmith will be able to see whether it fits properly by the brown marks the hot shoe will make on the wall of the hoof. He will be able to make any necessary alterations before plunging the shoe into a bucket of cold water to cool it down ready to be nailed. The nail ends, or clenches, are turned over and hammered down, and then tidied up with a rasp. If the nails are not driven in correctly they will pinch the foot or prick the laminae, causing blood poisoning or the formation of an abscess. The blacksmith will go over the shoe with a rasp to tidy up any rough edges and to make sure it fits snugly.

Shoes are more than plain semicircles of iron. They usually have clips to help hold them in position, and each shoe has a groove known as a 'fuller' running round the part that comes into contact with the ground to give it a better grip. Calkins, which are made by turning over the metal at the heel to form a small step, can also help to improve the foothold.

Horses used for competition work sometimes have shoes with screw holes in them to allow studs to be inserted. The studs, which can be of various shapes and sizes, enable the horse to get a better grip

when galloping and jumping or when going over a slippery surface. Leather pads can also be placed over the foot and held in place with the shoe to prevent the sole of the foot from becoming damaged or made sore by sharp flints and stones. The pads also help to absorb any additional shock when the ground is especially hard. They must, however, be removed at regular intervals.

The traditional shoeing technique of fitting a hot shoe to the horse's hoof is being replaced by cold shoeing methods. The traditional technique is the best, though when a blacksmith knows a horse well he is sometimes able to make a set of shoes in the forge that can be fitted cold.

SADDLERY

All saddlery should be kept in a dry place away from artificial heat, which will dry out the natural oils. Leather is badly affected by extremes of temperature and humidity because it becomes brittle when the temperature is too hot, and in a damp atmosphere absorbs water and becomes nasty and sodden. A warmish damp atmosphere will make the leather mouldy.

Leather has two sides, the grain and the flesh side. The grain side is waterproof, and the pores are closed in the curing process. They are left open on the flesh side to allow the leather to absorb nourishment, and it is this side that needs the greatest care during cleaning.

Tack should be taken completely to pieces for cleaning. Then a sponge wrung out in a bucket of tepid water can be used to remove particles of dirt and sweat, and after the leather has been allowed to dry, saddle soap or some other good leather dressing should be applied and rubbed well in to the flesh side. This will help to keep the leather supple and prevent it from becoming stiff when it gets wet. It will also help to preserve the stitching.

A well equipped and organized tack room. All saddlery needs to be regularly cleaned and carefully maintained to have a long life and be safe and comfortable to use.

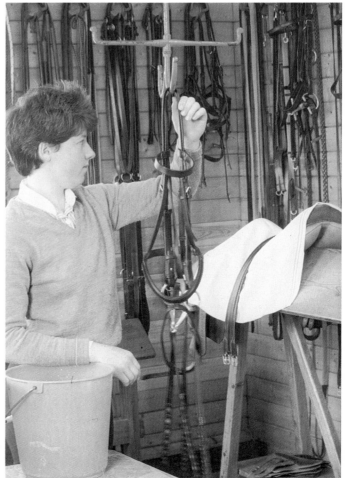

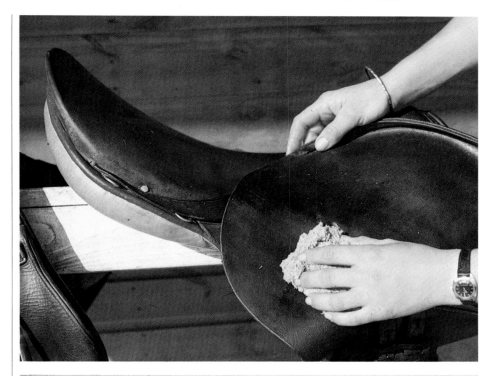

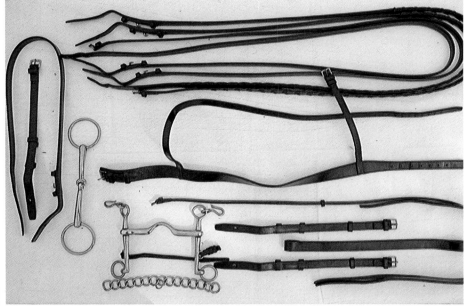

Top: Cleaning a saddle. The underside should be well cleaned to 'feed' the leather and keep it supple.

Above: The parts of a double bridle. Unless the bridle is stitched together, it should be taken to pieces for cleaning.

Opposite: Cleaning a bridle. The leather parts are washed and then rubbed with saddle soap; metal parts are best polished with a cloth after washing. Metal polish should not be used as horses dislike the taste.

Good quality, well cared for leather rarely breaks and will remain strong and supple for many years.

Metal items of saddlery such as buckles, bits and stirrup irons should be wiped clean and polished with a dry cloth, and the tongues of the buckles will need frequent oiling to prevent them from becoming too stiff.

The function of the bridle is to hold the bit in the horse's mouth. In addition to the bit the bridle is usually made up of five parts. The noseband is almost always included, though it is not an essential item; it is held in position by a strap passing over the poll and adjusted by a buckle on the near side. The noseband itself is fastened by a buckle at the rear.

The cheek pieces are attached at one end of the bit by means of buckles or stitching, and at the other end of the headstall by buckles. The headstall passes over the head and lies on top of the noseband headstrap. It is kept in place by the throatlash, which fastens round the throat by a buckle on the near side. The browband goes across the forehead, and has loops at either end through which pass the supporting straps of the noseband and the headstall for the bit. The reins are in two parts, and are held together by a central buckle. They are fixed to the rings of the bit by either a buckle or stitching.

The snaffle bridle has only five parts, but the double bridge has two headstalls and two additional cheek pieces, an additional pair of reins and a curb bit with curb chain and lip strap.

When a bridle is fitted the noseband should be adjusted so that it allows the breadth of two fingers below the cheek bone, and should be loose enough to admit at least two fingers between the nose bone and the jaw. The throatlash should not be tighter than is necessary to prevent the bridle from slipping forward over the ears, and loose enough for the breadth of the hand to be placed between it and the horse's lower jaw. The browband should fit comfortably enough to prevent the bridle from slipping backwards, but not be so tight that it will rub the horse's ears.

The use of the correct bit is essential if the horse is to be comfortable and remain properly under the rider's control. The sensitiveness of a horse's mouth will vary, and it is important to find out which type of bit is best suited to each animal.

When inexperienced riders have difficulty in controlling a horse they are often misled into believing that a more severe bit is the best answer to their problem. This is not usually the case, because the horse's usual reaction to pain is to pull harder, and in an effort to ease the pain and avoid the action of the bit he will either cross his jaw, throw up his head, lean on the bit, or put his tongue over it. Very often horses that tend to take a rather strong hold will go more kindly in a snaffle because it gives them less discomfort.

Not only must the correct type of bit be found but the one chosen must be the correct width for the particular horse's mouth, and the bridle should be adjusted until the bit just touches the corners of the mouth without wrinkling or drawing them up.

The snaffle is a single metal piece which goes upwards against the corners of the lips when the horse's head is low; it bears on the lower jaw and the tongue when the horse's head is high. There are a variety of

Putting on a bridle. The headcollar should be removed and fastened round the horse's neck while the bridle is being put on so that the horse remains safely under control. A horse will open its mouth to accept the bit if pressure is put by the thumb on the bars of the mouth. With the bit in place, the headpiece can be slipped over the horse's ears and the noseband and throat lash are fastened.

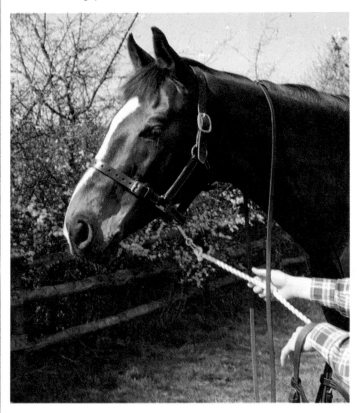

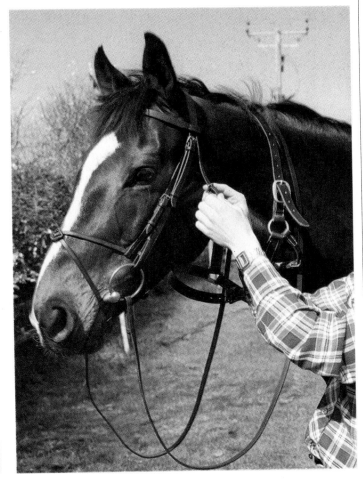

Some of the many types of bit available. *Right*: the different kinds of snaffle; *below left*: the bridoon and curb bits of a double bridle, with curb chain and lip strap; *below right*: a pelham; *bottom left*: a Kimblewick, *bottom right*: plain and padded curb chains

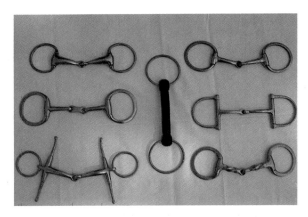

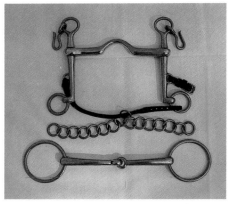

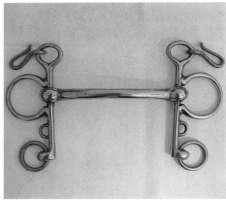

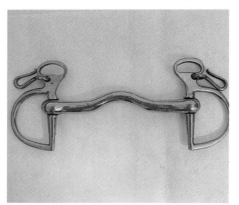

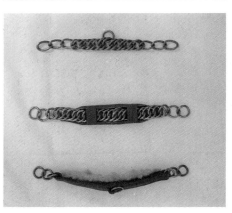

snaffle bits but the most popular are the eggbutt snaffle, the German snaffle, the Fulmer snaffle, the rubber snaffle, the twisted snaffle and the double jointed snaffle.

The double bridle consists of the bridoon, which is a thinner type of snaffle, and the curb bit, which provides additional control and makes possible more refined aids.

The pelham aims to combine the effect of a snaffle and a curb bit in one mouthpiece, and requires two reins. Leather roundings, which are curved couplings, are sometimes attached to the bridoon and curb rings on a pelham bit so that only one rein need be used.

The Kimblewick bit uses the principle of the roundings, but there is a single large metal 'D' running from above the mouthpiece to the bottom of the bit's cheekpiece.

Horses that have injured mouths may be ridden in a bitless bridle, which has no mouthpiece but exerts pressure on the nose and chin. The hackamore is the best-known type, in which two long metal cheeks are curved so that their leather attachments go across the nose and behind the chin when the rider pulls on the reins.

The type and shape of a saddle is a matter of personal taste and comfort, as well as varying according to the purpose for which the horse is being used. The requirements of any saddle are that it must not allow any weight to be placed on the horse's spine, nor press upon or pinch the withers. The weight must be evenly distributed and carried by the muscles on either side of the horse's backbone. Too broad a saddle will bear upon the spine and withers, while one that is too narrow will pinch the withers. When mounted the

Above: the right way to carry tack.

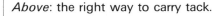

Right and opposite: How to put on a saddle; the girth should be loosely fastened at first and tightened up just before the rider mounts.

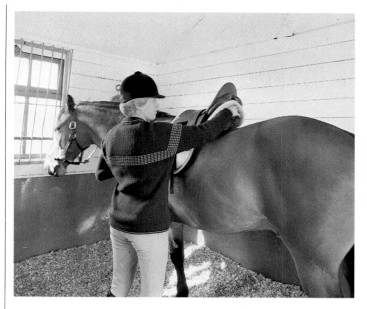

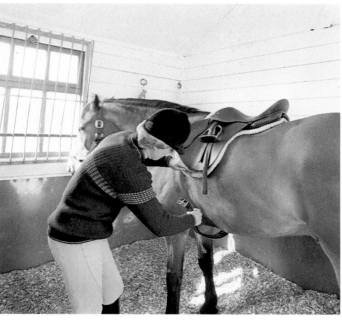

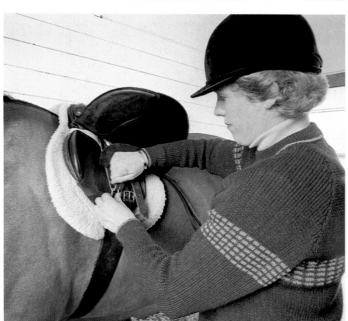

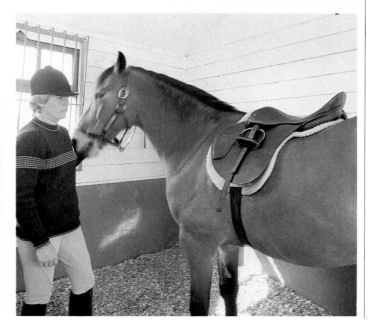

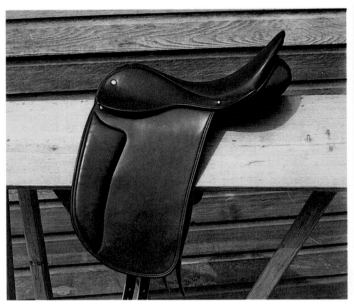

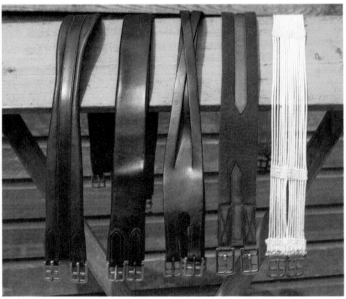

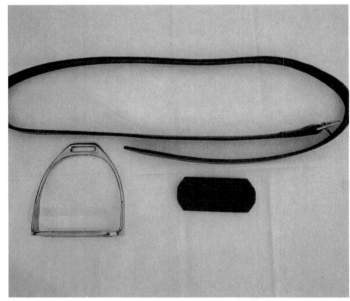

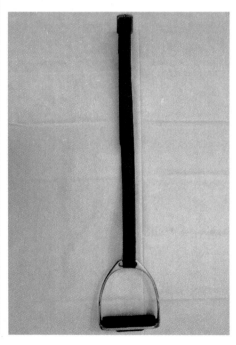

rider should be able to insert at least two fingers between the withers and the saddle front when he leans forward. The panels of a saddle must be well stuffed, because when the stuffing is insufficient or has become spread and thin with use there is a greater likelihood of the saddle pressing down upon the horse's back and withers.

Other important items of saddlery are a headcollar, which is usually made of leather and is used to tie up or lead the horse, or a halter which is used for the same purpose but is usually made of hemp or cotton, and rarely has a throat lash or buckles; a martingale, which may be used to help control the position of the horse's head; a breast plate, which helps prevent the saddle from slipping back; and a crupper, particularly useful with ponies, which is attached to the back 'D' of the saddle and passes under the tail to prevent the saddle from slipping forward.

Top row: the three principal varieties of saddle. An all-purpose saddle (*left*) is used for all ordinary riding; the dressage saddle (*centre*) has a straight-cut panel as longer stirrups are used to give extra leg contact and more subtle aids; for jumping, a saddle with a more forward-cut panel (*right*) is required.

Above left: Three kinds of leather girth, a webbing girth and, on the right, one made of nylon. Leather girths are the hardest wearing but should be used only with fit horses, not on animals in soft condition.

Above right and left: A stirrup iron and leather. Rubber treads help to prevent the foot slipping out of the iron, which should be wide enough to release the foot easily in the event of a fall.

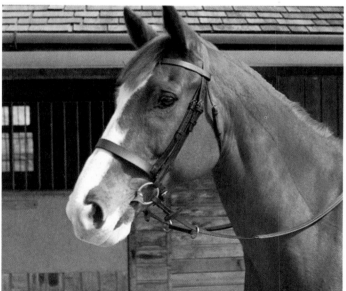

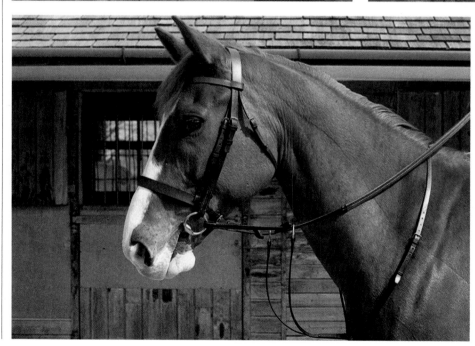

Martingales are widely used to help improve the head carriage. They are, however, no substitute for proper schooling.

The Irish martingale (*above left*) is a short strip of leather with a ring at each end, used mostly in racing to stop the reins going over the horse's head in a fall. A standing martingale (*above right*) is attached at one end to the girth, passes through the loop on the neckstrap and fixes on to a cavesson noseband. The running martingale acts on the horse's mouth; it divides after passing through the neckstrap, and the reins are threaded through rings on the ends. Both standing and running martingales should have a stop just above the point where they pass through the neckstrap, and stops should also be fitted to the reins near the bit with a running martingale.

HORSE CLOTHING

Because stabled horses cannot exercise themselves they will need rugs to keep them warm in winter and as a protection from the flies in the summer. The most common form of stable clothing is the night rug or stable rug, which is usually made from jute and blanketing. In the winter the rug can be used with a blanket. The heavy type of Yorkshire blanket is best, because two or three light ones not only take longer to put on but they are more likely to become loose and get trodden on and damaged when the horse lies down.

The blanket should be put on the horse's back lengthways from ear to tail, and drawn back slowly to smooth the hairs. Make sure it hangs down evenly on both sides. The front of the blanket can then be folded up on either side until it comes to a point over the horse's ears, and after the stable rug has been put in place, the front of the blanket can then be folded back over the withers on top of the rug to be held in place with a roller. Most rollers are about 5 in (12 cm) wide. The cheaper ones are made in webbing of wool, hemp or jute, and the more expensive are of leather.

There are a number of good proprietary brands of stable rug on sale which are made of materials other than jute. Some have their own surcingles in addition to a breast strap, but a separate roller can have the advantage of additional padding which will help to protect the vulnerable part of a horse's spine in the area behind the withers.

Good quality rugs are usually less expensive in the long run because they last longer and stand up much better to washing. Night rugs usually become dirty and stained and have to be cleaned at frequent intervals.

Rugs should always fit easily around the horse's neck so that he can lower his head to eat, but they should not be so loose that they can slip backwards and

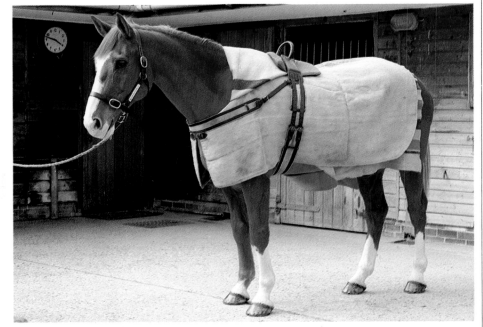

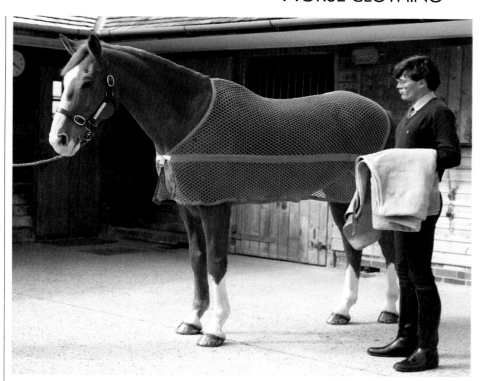

Opposite, above: A jute night rug over a blanket, and secured with an arched roller. The blanket should be folded back to fit under the roller so that it does not slip, and a pad is often used to give extra protection to the horse's withers.

Opposite, below: A day rug, edged with contrasting binding, is not strictly essential stable wear but does look smart.

Left: The anti-sweat sheet, widely used after competition work or on other occasions when a horse has been sweating after strenuous exercise or is wet from rain.

Below: Fitting the leg straps, which help to keep a rug in place.

chafe the withers. Rugs can be purchased in various sizes to ensure that they fit correctly. As they are particularly vulnerable to moths they should be stored in a suitably dry cupboard or chest, preferably with a few mothballs as a safeguard.

The amount of clothing the horse will need at night should be gauged by the lowest point of temperature reached before morning. A warm evening can quickly turn to a cold night, and it is always safer to rug a horse up well and leave the top of the stable door open so that he can get plenty of fresh air.

The horse's ears should always be warm right to their tips. If they are cold an extra blanket will be needed, and the ears should be massaged by gently pulling until they are warm. A horse that is too hot will sweat behind the ears.

Night rugs can also be used during the day without one of the night blankets. For travelling to competitions, however, day rugs do look smart. They are made of thick coloured woollen fabric trimmed with contrasting braid, and usually have the owner's initials sewn in one corner. Like the night rug they are held in place by a matching surcingle or roller. They also have eyelets at the rear for a threaded tail string, which helps to prevent the rug from slipping forward.

Summer sheets help to keep flies and dust away from the horse in the stable or when travelling. They are made of cotton or linen, and in addition to being held in place with a surcingle they also have a fillet string at the rear attached to loops at each corner to prevent the sheet from being blown about.

A New Zealand rug makes it possible for a clipped horse to spend at least some of its time out of doors whatever the weather. These rugs require regular maintenance to keep them fully waterproof and comfortable, and the leg straps must be kept soft and supple or they will chafe the horse's skin.

The horse's version of an anorak – the Lavenham rug. Though possibly less hard wearing than a New Zealand rug, it combines weather protection with warmth, and is light and comfortable for the horse.

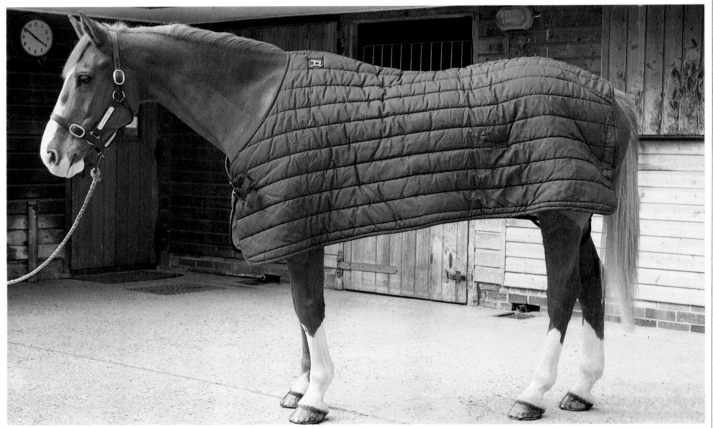

The anti-sweat sheet is a valuable asset in any stable. These are made of large cotton mesh, and work on the same principle as a string vest. By creating air pockets next to the horse's body they become a form of insulation which will prevent him from becoming chilled when he is wet from either rain or exercise. These rugs usually have to be used with a top sheet. Like all other rugs and sheets, they must be kept in place with a roller.

The New Zealand rug, which is usually made of stout canvas and lined with blanketing, is the only form of rug that can be used on horses turned out in a field. Being waterproofed, it provides good protection from wind and weather and enables a trace-clipped horse or pony to be wintered out quite happily.

The New Zealand rug is the same shape as a normal rug with one, or perhaps two, straps at the front secured by buckles. It has additional straps at the back, however, which cross over each other and pass round the horse's hind legs to hold the rug in position and stop it from becoming displaced when the animal rolls. Most New Zealand rugs also have a surcingle.

Because they are continually being brushed against branches and hedgerows, New Zealand rugs get hard wear and require constant attention. Any cuts or tears should be dealt with immediately to

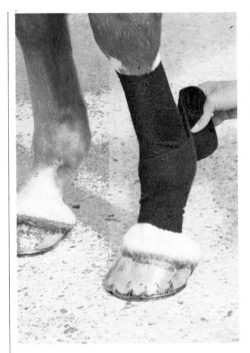
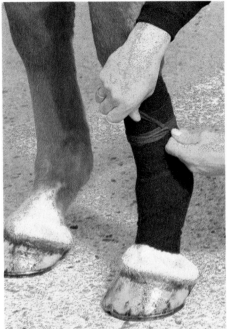
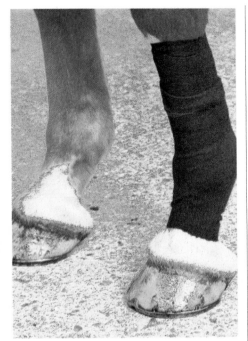

Stable bandages are used both in the stable for extra warmth and to help in the treatment of leg injuries, and when travelling. They should be put on firmly enough to be secure, but

not be so tight that the horse's circulation is impaired. The method is the same whether or not a layer of gamgee is used: the bandage is rolled down the leg and back up again, with

the tapes being fastened on the outside, never against the cannon bone or tendons.

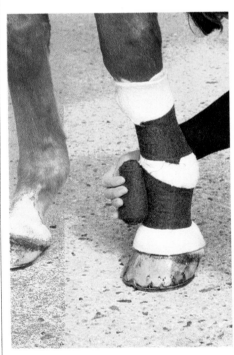
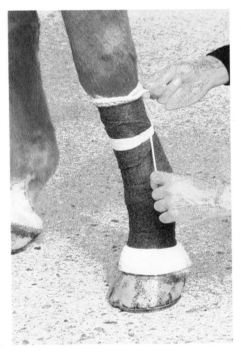
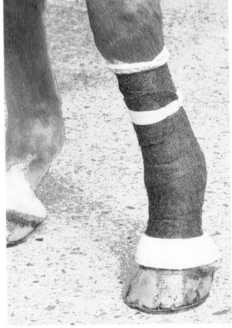

prevent rain from getting through to the warm blanketing, and the leather straps will need regular greasing to prevent them from getting too hard. The buckles and fastening hooks will also need to be oiled regularly.

Horses do not really need any other form of protective clothing when they are stabled, except for bandages which can be put on a cold horse to help him to get warm or used to keep a poultice or leg

dressing in place. There are, however, many other items of clothing that help to protect a horse against injury when he is travelling or taking part in various sports or competitions.

Two different types of bandages are used on the horse's legs. Stable bandages, which protect the horse when he is being transported, are made of woollen fabric or flannel about 3 in (8 cm) wide and 7 or 8 ft (2.25 m) in length. They have two tapes

at one end to hold the bandage in place.

To put on a stable bandage first make sure that it is neatly rolled with the tapes folded in the middle. It should then be applied to the leg, beginning just below the knee or hock, and wound downwards around the leg and fetlock joint as far as the coronet bone before being wound upwards again. The tapes are tied neatly below the knee, with the knot on the outside of the cannon bone and never on

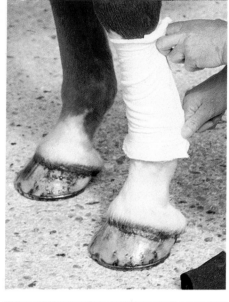

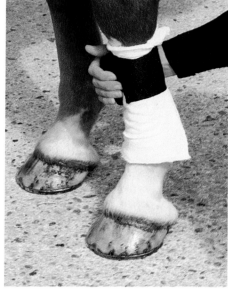

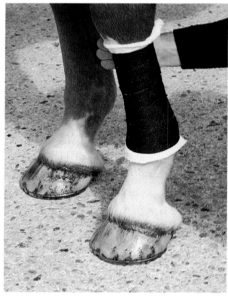

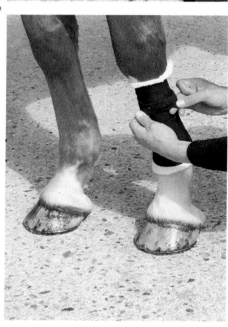

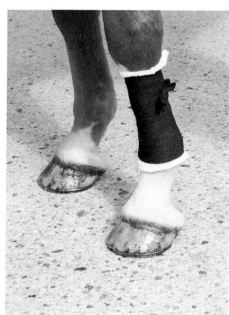

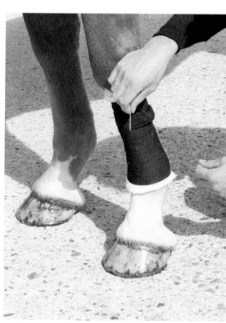

Exercise bandages support and protect the horse's legs during work, and must allow complete freedom of movement in the fetlock. They too must be put on firmly but not too tightly. It is particularly important to tie the tapes with care, and they are often sewn in place for work at speed over fences.

the tendons. Stable bandages must never be put on tightly but should be just firm enough to prevent them from slipping down. A layer of gamgee or foam rubber may be put under the bandage to give additional warmth and protection.

Exercise and working bandages, which have a degree of stretch, must always be put on over cotton wool or gamgee tissue. On the front legs working bandages are applied between the knee and the fetlock joint, and on the hind legs from just below the hock to the fetlock. They should be sewn in place for cross-country riding.

The tail bandage is another important bandage, particularly when a horse is travelling. It is a thin and flexible bandage which will prevent the top part of the tail from becoming damaged by rubbing against the box, and also improves the shape of the tail. To apply the tail bandage, first roll it up neatly with

the tapes folded inside. Dampen the hair, then unroll about 8 in (20 cm) of bandage. Holding the rolled up bandage in the right hand, put the loose end under the tail, holding it firmly in place. The tail should be held until the loose end can be secured by winding the bandage evenly down the tail. The bandage should then be wound back up the tail until it can be fastened with the tapes just below the top of the tail by using a double bow. The bow can be hidden by turning down part of the bandage. The tail bandage can be taken off quite easily by grasping it near the top and slipping it downwards over the tail with both hands.

There are various types of boots that are used to save a horse from injury. Knee caps and hock boots help to protect vulnerable areas. The knee cap consists of a strong leather pad, usually set in fabric. There is a well-padded leather strap at the

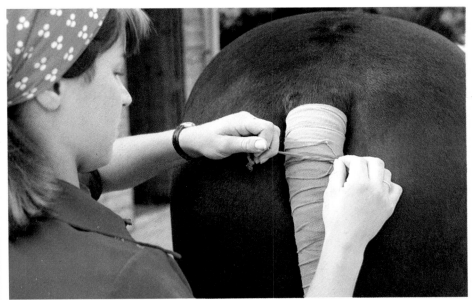

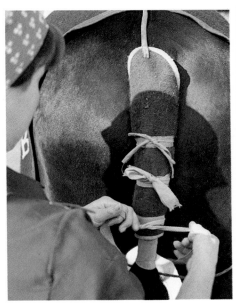

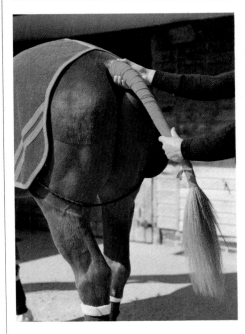

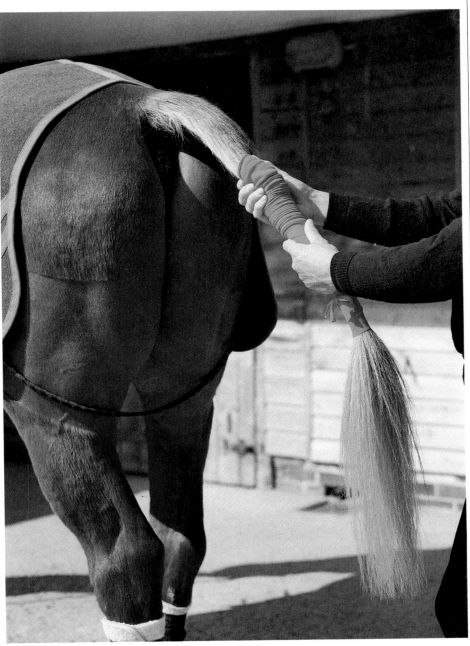

A tail bandage will improve the shape and appearance of both pulled and unpulled tails. A tail guard may be fitted over the bandage to prevent the horse rubbing it off, especially when travelling. The bandage is easily removed by sliding it down the tail.

Brushing boots and overreach boots (*above*) help to protect the horse's legs during exercise. Permanent lameness can result from injury to the knees, so knee caps (*above right*) can be useful, particularly if the horse does a lot of road work.

top that buckles fairly tightly above the knee and prevents the knee cap from slipping downwards.

The lower strap is buckled loosely below the knee in such a way that the joint can bend normally, and its function is to prevent the knee cap from turning upwards.

The hock boot is rather similar to the knee cap and is also fastened top and bottom by leather straps, but its main purpose is to prevent injuries to the hocks when the horse is travelling.

Various types of boots are used to save a horse from knocks and cuts when it is being ridden. The lighter type of five-strap felt or leather brushing boot gives good protection against occasional brushing when a horse hits one foreleg or hind leg against the other as he moves. The horse's fetlock can come into contact with the ground when he gallops or lands over a jump, and when that happens a boot covering the heel will save damage from flints and stones. Rubber overreach boots will also help to protect the horse from overreaches, when the front leg is struck by a hind hoof. A more damaging type of injury can occur when a horse strikes itself around the joint and at the back of the tendons, and to reduce this risk tendon boots should be used which are shaped to the leg and have a strong leather-covered pad at the rear.

TRAVELLING BY ROAD

A horse fully dressed for travelling. While few owners feel it is necessary to use all the items available, with a particular horse – one that is unusually restless, for example – it may be wise to offer some special protection.

Horses may be transported by road in a horse trailer, which has to be towed by another vehicle, or in a horsebox. Most horses will travel well provided that they have enough room, the vehicle has a suitable suspension, and they are being driven with reasonable consideration.

The number of rugs a horse needs when travelling will depend on the weather but horses generate a considerable amount of heat in a confined space and many sweat with excitement. Horses should always be bandaged, and knee caps and hock boots will help to prevent injury.

When loading a horse always look straight ahead and never at the horse and don't pull at him if he hangs back. When transporting a single horse put him on the side where he will be travelling on the crown of the road.

If a horse is reluctant to be loaded he should be encouraged with a feed or titbits, and there should be as much light as possible because a shy horse will sometimes load if he can see what is inside and there are no dark corners. Make the entrance as large as possible by moving one of the partitions to one side or taking it

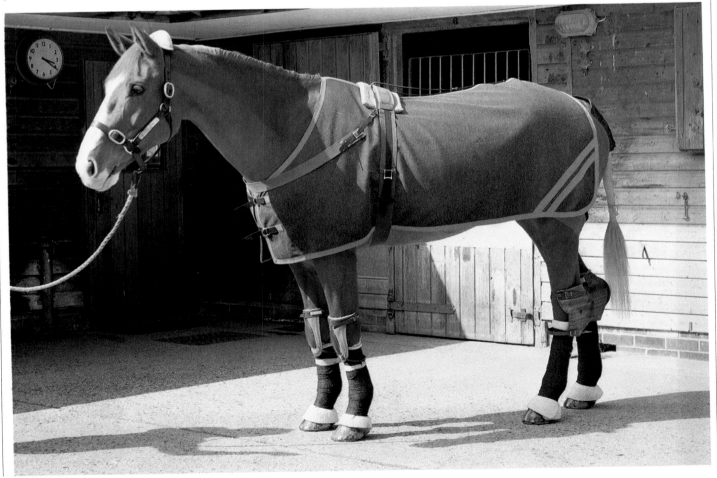

It is worth spending time teaching a horse to load without a fuss, and to familiarize it with the box or trailer it is useful to feed it there occasionally when no journey has to be undertaken. To unload, horses should be turned round and led calmly out; it is best never to back a horse down the ramp.

out altogether. If another horse is available he can be loaded first as a lead, or the horsebox or trailer can be pulled up alongside a wall to provide a 'wing' for loading. A steep ramp can be made much more tempting by backing the vehicle up against higher, level ground onto which the ramp can be lowered, and by spreading straw over the ramp.

Long reins can be fixed to the sides of the ramp with assistants to hold them taut. They can help to persuade a horse to keep straight, and as he starts to move forward the assistants can cross over keeping the reins taut and applying pressure on the horse's legs just above the hocks. As a final measure the horse can be led in blindfold.

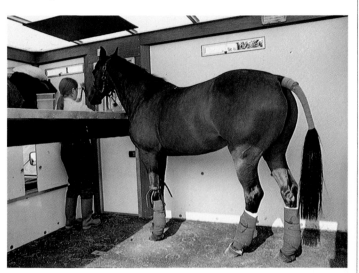

COMPETITIVE RIDING

Show jumping competitions are usually decided on the speed and manner in which a horse jumps the fences, so the layout of the course and the way in which the obstacles are built are of considerable importance, and the fences – even when big – should encourage the horse and rider to meet them with confidence. There is no set course or obstacle and the more important shows each have their own characteristics.

Courses generally vary in length from 500 to 900 yards (457 and 823 m). The track is the path which must be followed by the rider in order to complete the course. With the exception of banks each fence should require a horse to make one single jump or effort, and faults are always recorded at each fence. In the main the fences, although varied, will be divided into two categories – the upright fence and the spread fence.

An upright fence – such as gates, walls, post and rails, or a single rail – is built so that all the elements are placed vertical to the ground, and one above each other in the same plane. The heights will vary in order to create degrees of difficulty, while narrow fences such as a stile, a small wicket gate or short poles placed in a gap can be a greater test of the horse's obedience.

The spread fence is built to make a horse jump width as well as height. Among the most popular of the spread fences are the double oxer, the triple bars, the parallel bars, the hog's back and the water jump.

Horses need to learn to jump both upright and spread fences. Spreads are usually easier to jump, and with an inexperienced horse a ground line (a pole on the ground in front of the fence) should be used to help the horse judge the right point to take off, particularly over upright fences such as gates and rails.

Rails may be added to some upright fences to turn them into spread fences. As in the case of straight fences, the heights and spreads will vary considerably.

When two or more fences are placed so that they follow directly one after the other, and if the inside distance between any two does not exceed 39 ft 4 in (12 m), they will be regarded as a combination, and except in special cases will be regarded as one obstacle. Combinations should be included in all courses because they test the suppleness and obedience of a horse. The distances between the fences can vary. It may be a relatively simple combination, where there are one or two non-jumping strides between each element, or it may be a more difficult combination when the rider must decide how best to deal with the problem by asking the hose to lengthen or shorten his

stride by checking, decreasing or increasing his speed.

The distance between the fences will depend on the number of non-jumping strides required, and the height and nature of the fences and how they are placed. A non-jumping stride means the stride taken by a horse after landing and before taking off at the next fence, and the stride of a horse will vary according to its size and way of cantering. The average stride at the canter is usually taken to be about 10 ft (3 m), but it could be less if the horse is going slowly, or more if he is going faster. The height and nature of the fence will decide where the horse will take off and land. When jumping a small fence the horse will obviously not land as far away as when jumping a big fence, and in the case of a spread fence he will land further away still because he will be going faster

Jumping a combination fence. The horse approaches the first obstacle with good impulsion and control. There is room for one non-jumping stride between the two elements, and the horse must still have enough impulsion to take him safely out over the second element. Combinations may consist of two jumps (a double) or three (a treble).

in order to jump the distance of the spread.

Between two upright fences of, say, 4 ft (1.20 m) in height, the easy distance for a horse to be able to take one non-jumping stride would be 24 ft (7.30 m) and the distance for two non-jumping strides would be 33–36 ft (10–10.65 m). These distances can be varied on occasions according to whether the course is to be made more difficult, or perhaps a particularly simple course for novices.

If the combination is composed of a spread fence followed by an upright fence the distance should be increased to make the combination easier. The horse will have to approach the spread fence at a faster speed and will consequently land further out into the double. If, however, the first is an upright fence and the second part is a spread the distance between the fences should be reduced or the horse will have to reach for the second fence. If the competition calls for the horses to jump at speed the distances may be increased.

One of the most important differences between a show jumping track and a cross country course is the way in which the fences are constructed. Although a show jumping course should always include some natural-looking obstacles such as gates, rustic poles or perhaps fences made up with brush, all the obstacles in a show jumping ring must be built so that they can be knocked down. Cross country courses are built with fences that will not knock down. They are known as 'fixed' obstacles.

Cross-country riding requires a rather different approach from that needed in the confines of a show jumping arena. The fences are usually not only solid looking but fixed solid; the horse must be bold enough to jump in his stride at a hunting pace and also be clever and agile enough to cope with more awkward obstacles. This sequence shows a good, clean jump over an inviting obstacle.

Combination fences on cross-country courses take many forms, and there is often more than one route to choose from. The rider will select the best route for his own mount; a big, long-striding horse will be less well suited to tight turns or sharp changes in direction than a smaller, more agile animal with the scope for tackling the biggest fences. For this fence the rider has chosen to go straight across, jumping in and out again without any non-jumping strides between the two elements.

Time plays an important part in show jumping, particularly when there is a jump-off against the clock, but the speed at which a cross country course has to be jumped is fixed before the start of a competition. Some hunter trials have a 'bogey' time for the course based on the overall length, and competitors can be penalized for completing the course too quickly or too slowly.

As with show jumping, it is important for competitors to walk the course very carefully, taking note of the best approach to each fence bearing in mind the take-off and landing conditions, and the position of the next obstacle. It is as well also to take note of the weather; if it is a sunny day, for example, the sun may cast shadows across the approach to the jump by the time the competition starts, and the

shadows can cause a horse to spook or see a false ground line. Jumping a show jumping course will demand that horse and rider jump with speed and precision. The cross country course needs a different approach, because although the fences have to be jumped with a certain amount of speed and accuracy they need to be attacked with courage and obedience on the part of the horse, who will probably be asked to jump not only fences that he has not only not seen before but also when he cannot see where he is landing.

A one-day event or horse trials is a test in which the horse and rider have to compete in three different phases – dressage, show jumping and cross country. It is the all-round test of horse and rider; in order to do well the rider must be proficient in all three disciplines, and the

Above: To compete successfully across country a horse must be a bold jumper with faith in his rider, and be prepared to tackle any obstacle however strange it may seem. This horse may never have met beer barrels before, but is jumping with great confidence and style.

Left: One of the features of this fence is that the horse must jump into shadow, as well as negotiating the various elements of the jump itself.

horse must combine agility, speed, stamina, and jumping ability, with obedience. There are competitions at different levels according to each horse's experience and the number of points which he has won. One-day events vary in standards of difficulty, while it is the three-day event that places the greatest demands on both horse and rider. It was originally a competition to test the stamina and versatility of military chargers, and the first international competition was at the Stockholm Olympics in 1912 when, contrary to modern practice, the dressage phase was held on the last day. One-day horse trials, in which all the tests usually take place on the same day, evolved as practice competitions for the three-day events. They still do to a certain extent, and they enable young horses and riders to gain experience before tackling the more rigorous three-day competitions.

All events are judged on a points system, and the penalty points are cumulative over the three phases. Penalty points awarded for the dressage are added to those gained for refusals, falls, or exceeding the time limit on the cross country, and penalties can also be gained in the show jumping phase for exceeding the time limit as well as for knock downs and falls.

Dressage tests at one-day events vary according to the class, but the same dressage test is used at all senior international three-day events. It has to be ridden from memory and although it is not judged by the same rigorous standards as the advanced tests in pure dressage the horses have to be sufficiently advanced in their schooling to carry themselves correctly and to perform the different movements of the test competently, calmly, and obediently.

The speed and endurance tests take place on the second day. They vary in length, and the size of the fences can also differ according to the calibre of the competition. Distances of up to 15 miles (24 km) have to be covered at set speeds, and in the Olympics the distance can be extended to up to about 18.6 miles (30 km). The distance is divided into four phases, the first of these being the roads and tracks, followed by the steeplechase course, then more roads and tracks, and finally the cross country course.

The cross country is the exciting centrepiece of three-day and one-day events, and the course builders need flair and imagination as well as the necessary experience to understand fully the extent of the problems to set horse and rider. Big, straightforward fences on good open ground are usually less likely to cause difficulty to a bold and agile horse than

Top: The bullfinch also demands courage from both horse and rider, as it has to be jumped through rather than over.

Above: The dressage phase of a one- or three-day event may be less spectacular, but is an important part of the competition.

some of the problem fences, which can be deceptive and sometimes appear less formidable to the inexperienced rider than they really are.

A combination of fences set at awkward distances apart; landings with a drop the horse cannot see; jumping into water where the bottom is not visible; deep, dark ditches; banks and rails without a stride –

all these place considerable demands on a horse's courage. The rider has to convince the horse that what lies ahead is safe and negotiable, and he is being asked to jump the obstacle in the easiest way. It is this confident partnership between horse and rider that is the essence of good cross country riding.

On the final day of a three-day event the horses have to pass a veterinary inspection before they are allowed to take part in the last phase – the show jumping. The object of the show jumping is to prove that the day after a severe test of endurance the horses have retained their suppleness and have the energy and obedience necessary for them to continue. The show jumping course is not intended to be particularly demanding, and a clear round is usually vital as one fence knocked down can mean a change in the final order.

Good event horses come in all shapes and sizes. Many good eventers are not Thoroughbreds, and some are hardly bigger than ponies. They must, however, all have courage and stamina and be sufficiently level headed for the dressage. They must enjoy jumping and have the scope to jump big fences out of a galloping stride, yet be intelligent enough to respect the fences.

BUYING A HORSE

Choosing a suitable horse to buy is a matter of judgement and a little luck. It is important to be realistic in assessing one's ability, aspirations and circumstances before starting to look for the right animal, and inexperienced riders should ask for help in finding a suitable purchase.

The choice of a suitable horse must depend on a number of factors. First there are the ambitions and experience of the rider to be considered. A young Thoroughbred would hardly be a suitable mount for a learner, but it may be an ideal purchase for someone who has the necessary experience to train a horse for competition work. The facilities available and the time an owner has for looking after the horse are two more important considerations. Thoroughbreds need to be stabled if they are going to do well, whereas a less well-bred animal can often be turned out with a New Zealand rug in

the winter months, and provided that he is fed correctly and given the necessary amount of attention, he will be able to do a reasonable amount of work without requiring as much time spent on him as a stabled horse.

Having decided on the type of horse it is important to have a clear indication of the age you would like it to be and the amount of money available. Age is important because although younger animals usually have more years of useful work ahead of them, they are likely to be inexperienced and will need a certain amount of training. A novice rider is more

likely to learn from a well-schooled older horse.

These decisions should be made before setting out to find the right animal. Horse sales are not the best places for the inexperienced to look unless they are accompanied by an expert who will be able to judge the suitability of the various horses being auctioned. Many of the horses being sold at sales are covered by a warranty, but there are other factors to be taken into account which would not be covered by the warranty.

A safer way is to advertise in one of the equestrian magazines setting out exactly the type of animal required and perhaps asking for a photograph. With that method it is possible to start by seeing the horses nearest home and trying them under more relaxed conditions. It would again be wise to take an experienced and knowledgeable person to see and perhaps try the horse unless you really feel capable of making a wise choice.

The more experienced you are the easier it is to minimise the risks, but it is always wise to remember that a horse which may seem to be ideal when he is ridden in familiar surroundings at his owner's premises may prove very different when you get him home. Temperament as well as ability is extremely important – you may be able to alter a horse's bad habits by skilful schooling, but you will never be able to make significant changes to his temperament.

If you are lucky a friend may know of just the right animal to suit all your requirements, but finding the right horse usually calls for patience, careful searching, wise judgement, sensible vetting and preferably a thorough trial.

Always insist on seeing the horse being ridden by the owner or somebody who will ride it on his behalf before riding it yourself. If it has any bad habits it is better to know what to expect before finding yourself on the receiving end of trouble.

Much can also be learned of a horse's temperament when he is in his stable. They vary just as much as people and it always pays to spend a few minutes making friends before getting on his back. Approach him quietly and unhurriedly, preferably with a few well-chosen words and possibly a titbit. Begin by a pat on the neck rather than by handling him around the ears. Some horses are inclined to be shy and touchy about the head, and can quickly be upset. The horse will then have time to sum you up, and his reactions when you do get into the saddle will be more likely to be based on confidence.

It is as well to remember that a well-bred horse is a highly strung and nervous animal with more intelligence than many people give him credit for. He is quick to react not only to his rider's wishes but also to his temperament, and a nervous person will communicate his nervousness to the animal. That being the case, to obtain the best results the rider should approach the horse in a quiet, gentle, yet positive and confident manner.

Horses are usually willing to please if they can be made to understand exactly what is required of them. This anxiety to please when combined with confidence in the rider will lead a horse to overcome his own natural nervousness and highly developed sense of self-preservation in order to obey his rider's wishes.

This fine-looking horse would not be cheap either to buy or to care for, but properly looked after should help a rider to achieve considerable success.

Below: When choosing ponies for children it is particularly important to be sure of their temperament and disposition. Some ponies have great character, which will add to the pleasure they give their owners, but a spoilt or mean pony will be no fun to look after and could even be dangerous.

Bottom: The stage of development of the horse's teeth gives a reasonably accurate indication of its age.

If you can get the horse's confidence when you go to try him he will give you a better ride, and therefore a better indication of whether he is the sort of animal you are looking for and would be prepared to purchase.

Having made up your mind that he is the right type and would be suitable, and having checked as far as you can that he seems sound in wind and limb, it is always advisable to ask whether you can have him checked by a vet. Doing so can prevent a lot of problems later on, and it is important to know whether a potential purchase has any faults which may

prevent him from doing the work you may want him to do. Find a veterinary surgeon with good experience with horses and tell him exactly what you are looking for. He will not necessarily be qualified to comment on the price, but he will be able to tell you, for example, whether or not a horse will be able to stand up to the rigours of show jumping or eventing. He will also be able to tell you whether he has any faults which would preclude him from doing well in the show ring if you were hoping to show him. A few unsightly bumps and blemishes may not have any effect on his jumping or dressage ability, but they could put paid to his chances of doing well as a show horse.

As long as a horse is not too old a veterinary surgeon will be able to confirm its age fairly accurately, but that is something you should know how to do for yourself.

The age of a horse is determined by reference to the front incisor teeth. There are six of these teeth in each jaw, and like people, during its lifetime a horse has two complete sets, known as the milk teeth and the permanent teeth. Milk teeth are small and white with a distinct neck and short fang, whereas the permanent teeth are of a browner, yellowish colour. They are also much larger and do not have any distinct neck to them.

The changeover from the milk teeth to permanent teeth takes place at certain times and 'ageing' of a horse is based mainly on this fact, combined with the following indications:

A yearling has six new unworn milk teeth in each jaw.

A two-year-old still has a complete set of milk teeth but they will have become worn.

A three-year-old will have had the two centre milk teeth replaced by permanent

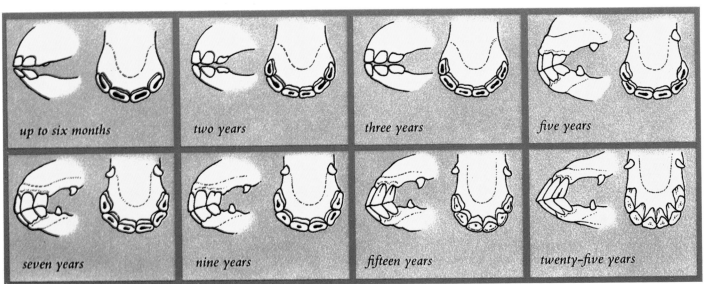

up to six months

two years

three years

five years

seven years

nine years

fifteen years

twenty-five years

When buying a horse it is valuable to have a veterinary inspection carried out to make sure that the horse is healthy and sound. The vet will check the horse in detail, listen to its heart and lungs before and after exercise, look at the way it moves when being ridden and when being led in hand. He will note any blemishes that might lead to soundness problems, and will be able to advise on whether a horse is suitable for the particular activities the purchaser has in mind.

teeth, which are larger and will show a sharp edge.

A four-year-old will have had two more milk teeth in each jaw replaced with permanent teeth, and a stallion or gelding will have a tush behind the corner incisor.

A five-year-old will also have lost the corner milk teeth, and new shell-like teeth will be visible at the corners.

A six-year-old will have a full mouth of permanent teeth but the corner teeth will have lost their shell-like appearance.

A seven-year-old will have a hook on the top corner tooth (a thirteen-year-old may show a similar hook).

An eight-year-old will have lost the hook but the tables of the teeth will begin to show signs of wear and the black hollow centres will have disappeared.

From nine years of age it is far more difficult to be sure of a horse's age, but a veterinary surgeon will be able to form an opinion by a knowledge of the changes in the outline of the tables of the teeth and the slope of the jaws.

It is also important to know the exact height of a horse, particularly if it is a show horse or, in the case of ponies, also a show jumper. The standard measurement of height for a horse is the 'hand', which is the equivalent to 4 in (10 cm). Only Shetland ponies are measured in inches; in future all standard measurements are likely to be given in centimetres as well as in hands. Measurement is made from the ground to the highest point of the withers; and a horse that is 66 inches or 5 ft 6 ins high, for example, is referred to as being 16 hands 2 in (often abbreviated to 16.2 h.h.). A horse is usually 15 hands or more in height; to compete as a pony an animal must usually not exceed 14.2 hands.

When you have found a horse or pony that is the right size and age, and appears to have the right experience, ability and temperament, before deciding to have him vetted take a final look and ask yourself these questions:

Does he really appeal to you, and has he a bold, kind and generous outlook? Horses with a bump between the eyes are often wilful and stubborn.

Is he well built with the various parts of his body in proportion?

Does he look intelligent and alert?

Does he move well with a good stride?

Has he got good bones and good joints?

Has he got good feet that do not turn inwards, and have walls which are smooth and free from rings and grooves?

If the answer to all these questions is 'yes', there is a good chance that you will be buying the right animal.

INDEX